SALENTO BY 5

Friendship, Food, Music, and Travel
Within the Heel of Italy's Boot

Audrey Fielding
THE TRAVELER

Luciana Cacciatore
THE RACONTEUR

Carlo Longo
THE MUSIC MAKER

David Fielding
THE SKETCHER

Lucia Erriquez
THE COOK

GEMELLI PRESS

Requests for permission to make copies of any part of the work should be submitted online at www.gemellipress.com/contact or mailed to the following address:

Gemelli Press
9600 Stone Avenue North
Seattle, WA 98103.

ISBN 978-0-9864390-8-7

Library of Congress Control Number: 2016950339

TABLE OF CONTENTS

Chapter One: Audrey

Chapter Two: Luciana

Chapter Three: David

Chapter Four: Carlo

Chapter Five: Lucia

Audrey says: *Salento is almost never identified on maps of Italy, and there is even disagreement among Salentinians as to its specific borders. Generally, however, it occupies the peninsula portion of the region of Puglia that forms the heel of Italy's boot, with its northern border formed by a line between the cities of Brindisi on the Adriatic Sea and through the town of Manduria and to the Ionian Sea. The distance across Salento varies from about thirty to forty miles, so people are used to traveling from one side to the other. Local roads often take you through many small towns, making it easy to get lost, but once you take the time to get familiar with the signs and are not shy about asking for help, you will find your way.*

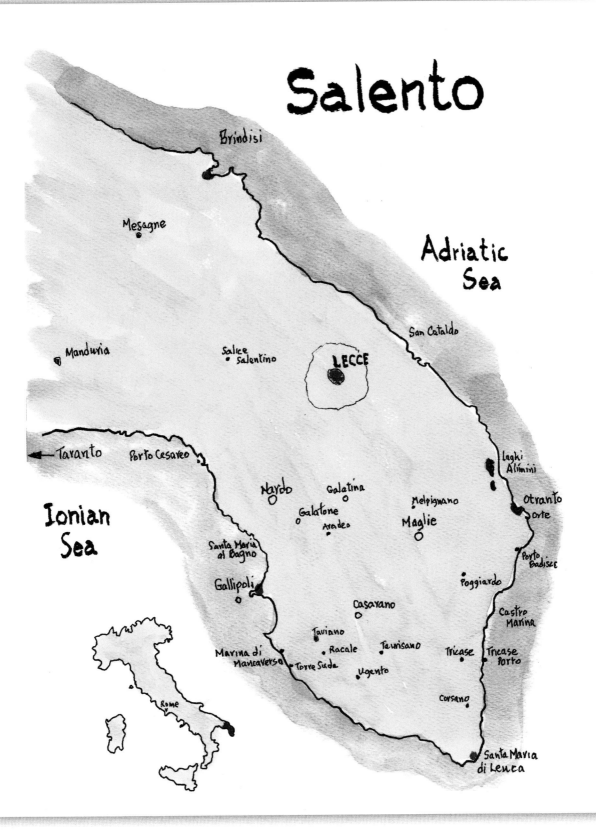

AI NOSTRI LETTORI ITALIANI.

Gli autori di *Salento by 5: Amicizia, Buona Cucina, Musica e Itinerari nel Tacco dello Stivale* sono lieti e onorati che voi abbiate acquistato questo libro, scritto per lo più in inglese, ma qua e là anche in salentino, o che siate orientati a farlo. Nella speranza di potervi offrire al più presto la versione italiana, nel frattempo vi diciamo che leggendo queste pagine potrete conoscere una parte –piccola, ma incredibilmente bella- dell'Italia Meridionale e che resterete ammaliati da storie e immagini che vi condurranno a nutrire la nostra stessa passione per il Salento, una terra da amare senza limiti.

Buona lettura!

A NOTE TO OUR ITALIAN READERS:

The authors of *Salento by 5: Friendship, Food, Music, and Travel Within the Heel of Italy's Boot* are pleased and honored that you have purchased or are considering the purchase of this book written mainly in English. We hope to offer you an Italian version in the near future. In the meantime, you have an opportunity to read and learn about a small but lovely part of southern Italy. The stories and illustrations will charm and enlighten you with the histories and passions of its authors as they express their love for the Salento. Happy reading!

Audrey Fielding
David Fielding
Luciana Cacciatore
Carlo Longo
Lucia Erriquez

THE AUTHORS

Audrey, The Traveler, *captures the enchantment of the Adriatic and Ionian Seas, the whisper of wind in the olive groves, and the tastes of earthy greens, ear-shaped pasta, and bowls of steaming mussels.*

Luciana, The Raconteur, *writes about her family and the trials of landownership and cultivation, contrasting the past with the present.*

Carlo, The Music Maker, *discovers the roots of his band's music in the stone-filled, ancient fields where peasants toiled and called to one another.*

David, The Sketcher, *evokes with his pen, ink, and watercolors impressions and recollections of Salento's picturesque towns, its seas, its olive trees, and more.*

Lucia, The Cook, *shares recipes and memories of growing up surrounded by the aromas of freshly baked bread and holiday sweets that permeated the air of her home and neighborhood in the small town of Taviano.*

PROLOGUE

Heel to Heel

It was both odd and serendipitous that I met a woman with a broken high heel in the Rome airport. In perfect English, she asked me to watch her luggage while she searched for someone to fix it. In a few minutes, a janitor offered help, laughing as he slammed the shoe against the wall. *Ecco fatto!* Done! In rapid-fire Italian, they joked. Then she and I headed off to our gates, only to find ourselves facing each other as we stood in a double line. We smiled politely and proceeded to check in at the desk. I was traveling to a work assignment in Africa via Dubai. She was a travel agent going to an exotic resort outside of Dubai. It seemed natural to sit next to each other in the waiting area and chat. When I told her that I would meet my husband in Rome on my way back from southern Africa and we would be traveling to Puglia in southern Italy, she announced, "I'm from Puglia. And you must take the train to Lecce. Driving will take too long. Here's my card. Come and see me." From the heel of a shoe to the heel of Italy's boot. What could be a more auspicious sign for a traveler than that?

Part travelogue, part cookbook, and part memoir, *Salento by 5* offers the reader a glimpse into the culture and history of Salento through the insights of three native Pugliese teachers and two American tourists without a guidebook and with little real knowledge but plenty of misconceptions about Italy's geography.

The first Italian narrator is Salento native Luciana, the woman with the broken heel in the Rome airport, the daughter of two teachers. After years of studying languages and living abroad, she returned to her hometown to teach. The second author is Carlo, Luciana's former high school English teacher, hometown neighbor, and distant relative. Carlo spent numerous summers in Salento with his grandparents, as a boy visiting from Liguria, and chose to live in Salento after graduating from college with a degree in English. Lucia, Carlo's wife, is the third narrator, and she teaches high school English. Carlo and Lucia met when he became her English tutor as she prepared for her university exams.

My work at the time I met Luciana was as an educational consultant advising English teachers on ways to improve reading and writing in the classroom. I had been an English teacher in San Francisco for over twenty years. What good fortune it was to meet three Italian teachers of English! My husband, David, was a lawyer who had closed his practice ten years earlier and had begun to explore an interest in drawing and sketching.

During our first years traveling to southern Italy, the two of us rambled along Salento's country lanes through olive tree groves, swam anywhere, anytime, and socialized with our English-speaking Italian friends. Over time, the place seemed to penetrate into the marrow of our bones. We returned to it annually and began to wonder why. We had no Italian relatives, only a casual interest in Italian food, and a fluency in Spanish that interfered with learning Italian. Our close friends wondered what kept us going back to the same place year after year. Weren't we bored with it by now? Surely the clear and clean seas and the rich red of the iron-filled soil all played a part in luring us back to Salento, but the more I thought about it, it was our Italian friends, Luciana, Lucia, and Carlo, who enticed us with food, stories, music, and books.

So why not write a book together with our Italian friends? A book that would explore the area, reveal the lives of the Italians, and share what it was like to be a traveler returning year after year? Carlo said, "Yes, like *The Canterbury Tales*, we will each tell our stories."

And so the idea of the book collaboration was born. It would become a collection of thoughtful essays written by local Italians sharing insights into the music, food, history, and culture of Salento. As the American traveler, my job was to provide context and integrate the narrative. David, as the artist, would provide sketches and pages from his journal to complement the text. The book would be a collection of stories, memories, and adventures for either the vicarious or actual traveler. Each writer would write from his or her point of view while the artist would draw evocative sketches of place. I would be The Traveler; David, The Sketcher; Luciana, The Raconteur; Carlo, The Music Maker; and Lucia, the Cook.

The five of us have been working collaboratively on this project for the past five years, staying in touch like the southern Italian fieldworkers of the 1940s, '50s, and '60s, who called to each other early in the morning for support, reassurance, and solidarity while tending their plots of land. Meanwhile, though some of our favorite places in Salento have changed, one can still walk along sheep and goat trails beside the Adriatic Sea in late spring, inhale the scents of rosemary, myrtle, and thyme, or watch wildflowers drooping with bees mining nectar while a morning sun glitters white on the sea, and time seems endless and enduring. *Salento by 5* is a joint effort to capture those scenes and to share and promote the deep satisfaction of cross-cultural friendships developed over time in a beautiful place with a rich history.

As coordinator of this book project, I have been challenged by the exciting yet delicate task of editing and melding the writing of five different authors, three of whom are Italian teachers of English writing in their non-native language. The goal has been to preserve the unique voice of each author. From the beginning, the five authors have wanted to share what they know and love about Salento in a format that would please the traveler on the road or in an armchair. I hope the stories entertain and educate. More broadly, I hope they inspire the reader to travel, study new languages, meet local people, and in the end, write together.

If stories show us how to live in the world, then we, as authors of this book, have done our part.

CHAPTER ONE

Audrey

THE TRAVELER

I was born in a small town in Connecticut and spent a good part of my youth wishing I were elsewhere. I escaped when and where I could to the houses and dinner tables of our Italian neighbors, the Testas and the Balderaccis, where meals were more interesting than the tuna casseroles and canned vegetables at my family's dinner table. Summer church camp never lasted long enough. Begging to stay overnight at friends' and relatives' homes was a constant irritant to my mother, who wanted me home. My relatives and neighbors, like wardens, made sure I went to school and church and behaved myself. For years, my aunt and uncle saved family antiques in the attic for when I would finally come home, marry, and settle down, perhaps in the colonial house just down the street. But I couldn't wait to grow up and leave. Thanks to President John F. Kennedy and the creation of the Peace Corps, I did just that as soon as I could.

The Peace Corps application I picked up at my hometown post office in 1961 represented my ticket to see the world. In college I majored in Spanish and minored in Sociology. Three weeks after college graduation in 1964, I was on my way to Peace Corps training in San Diego, California. My first plane flight was from Connecticut to Southern California, nonstop. I wore a yellow linen suit with a striped silk blouse and red flats. My hair, the part that flopped in a wave on my forehead, was bleached blond with peroxide. In my hands I carried a small white travel case, popular at the time, and my violin. I was twenty years old, scared, thrilled, and traveling at last. A few months later, our Peace Corps training group met up at LaGuardia in New York City for the Pan American flight to Lima, Peru, where we volunteers would receive our two-year assignments.

I met my husband, David, in the Peace Corps, and we married in Peru. We promised each other that even after graduate school and children we would continue to explore and live in other countries. So, after Peace Corps, law school, and graduate school in education, we spent two years in Calexico, California, on the border with Mexico, and then four years living and working in San Jose, Costa Rica, where I was a teacher and David worked as a Legal Fellow with the law school and the municipal government. In 1975, we returned to the United States, having rejected the expatriate life. I went back to school, David joined a law firm, and our two children entered public school and wondered when were we going "back home" to Costa Rica. But we were in San Francisco to stay, at least for a while. Travel would take place during summer vacations.

It was in 1992 that I received a teaching sabbatical year for travel and elected to go to Perugia, Italy, to study Italian. A friend of a friend had an apartment in the old section of the city that was available for a reasonable rent. I would take classes at the Università per Stranieri (University for Foreigners) for three months.

Although I was fluent in Spanish, the melodic lilt of the Italian language in that first Italian class seduced me. I couldn't understand much of what was being said, but it didn't matter. Understanding would come later.

In 1996, I returned to Italy to study Italian and live in Bologna, this time with my husband. While there, a classmate passed along a book about the women of southern Italy, *Women of the Shadows*, a sociological study of the lives of five women in southern Italy in 1926. In the book's introduction, author Ann Cornelisen writes, "The South is *not* the gentle terraced landscape of Renaissance painting. It is a bare, sepia world, a cruel world of jagged, parched hills, dry river beds and distant villages where clumps of low houses cling together on the edges of cutbanks."

I wanted to go there. I was sure that few tourists ventured that far south. So for years I told people I wanted to visit southern Italy, somewhere near the heel, a place called Puglia. I was intrigued by the descriptions in Cornelisen's book: strong and stoic women, simple and rustic food, stark and strangely beautiful geography.

But years later, when I finally arrived in Puglia, I found a different southern Italy. No hills, no bareness, and no clumps of houses clinging to cliffs. The southern Italy I have come to know is more diverse and prosperous than I could have imagined. It was not Ann Cornelisen's Italy but a different piece of the mosaic that makes up Italy's South. It was Salento, and it was here that my friendship began with Luciana, Carlo, and Lucia, Italians all and teachers of English.

I was a teacher consultant, a specialist in writing instruction, so our early conversations were about the role of writing in teaching literature, the challenges of English and Italian grammar, and the latest popular American idioms. On a visit to Lucia's classroom we found Italian students to be consumers of popular Southern California television programs, such as *Baywatch* and *The O.C.* My husband and I, non-TV watchers, were unable to answer their questions, though we did find common ground in talking about Barack Obama, who was soon to win the presidential election.

Back home in the States, our friends and family, puzzled by our visits every year to this distant part of Italy, asked us, "Are you going to Salento *again*? How many times have you been?" I have lost count over the years, and I can't imagine not returning as long as I am able to travel. Some places are like that. This collaborative book, rooted in friendship, has grown visit by visit, meal by meal into a rich tree of travel stories.

"Going to Salento again?" Book in hand, I'll nod yes, and here's why.

FRIENDS, FOOD, AND WINE

Salento is the warm womb of Mother Earth. It is heat and water and salt and iron-filled dirt. Think of things round (bosoms, olives, grapes, melons, tomatoes) and rippling (the abs on young Italian men at the seashore, the shimmer of wind on water and olive leaves).

This is Salento.

Like many Italians, Salentinos kiss on both cheeks and send you *baci* (kisses) and *abbracci* (hugs) from afar. They sit you down at their dinner tables late in the summer night and feed you mussels, almonds, pears, and pastries until you are drunk with satisfaction. But there are edges too—sharp rocks that scrape against your feet as you make your way to the sea, stinging jellyfish lurking in rocky coves, and cutting winds that swoop in from the north or south and stay for days to taunt and madden.

This, too, is Salento.

The first time we arrived in Puglia, after a six-hour train ride from Rome to Lecce, we had no idea where we would stay. A kind taxi driver saw us standing alone with our luggage outside the train station. I remember feeling so happy to be off the train. We had been surrounded by a group of Italian teenagers on holiday. Their incessant chatter, flirting, and jumping over seats had numbed our senses. Once outside the station, people disappeared. We basked in the silence until a taxi driver approached us.

What hotel were we going to?

Did we need help?

A ride?

We had no guidebook; we had no idea where to go. Oh, it really wasn't so alarming—we were seasoned travelers and we spoke some Italian. And so our adventure began.

On that quiet Sunday evening in July, our taxi driver led us to a room at a bed and breakfast in an old palazzo in the historic center of the southern, baroque city of Lecce. We stayed three days, roaming the cobblestoned streets of this university town, often lost until friendly young people guided us back to our palazzo. On early morning walks, the light off sandstone buildings caught the morning sun, bathing us in warmth. Flowering plants and twisted green tendrils hung from wrought iron balconies. The narrow streets were silent. But when we approached fancy clothing stores, newspaper kiosks, and coffee bars, delivery trucks, cars, scooters, and motorcycles startled us from behind or headed right for us. We ducked into doorways. We pressed our backs into walls. By early afternoon, everything settled down. It was lunch and *riposo* (rest) time.

Audrey says: *Many of Lecce's centrally located lodgings are comfortable bed and breakfast (B&B) establishments converted from old palaces or villas. My favorite B&B in Lecce is called* **Bed and Breakfast Prestige**. *It is located in the historical center on the upper floor of a Renaissance building. Breakfast is served on a sun porch with a view of the nearby Basilica del Rosario. Its rooms are immaculate and bright. Renata, the hostess, is friendly and speaks English.*
Info: www.bbprestige-lecce.it

In the heat of the day, we tourists wandered the streets past open windows, hearing the scrape of silverware against plates, the clinking of glasses, and always the drone of television. Except for *trattorie* (small restaurants) and coffee bars, businesses closed and remained that way until late afternoon. Then, small shops, one by one, began reopening their doors. By early evening people were outside, talking, walking, and eating gelato. Late into the evening, crowds flowed back and forth on the main street. Voices rose to a crescendo like a windstorm making its way up a narrow river canyon. An occasional police car, lights flashing, wove through the crowds. Cyclists walked their bikes while tourists ogled ornate baroque church facades, teenagers flirted, grandparents window-shopped, mothers pushed babies in elaborate strollers, fathers held the hands of little children, and immigrant Senegalese vendors spread their wares on bright African cloth, encouraging everyone to buy a trinket or two.

By our third day in Lecce, we skillfully maneuvered the city streets and began to plan our reunion with Luciana, the woman from Puglia I had met in the Rome airport a few weeks earlier as we awaited a flight to Dubai. I had been on my way to a teaching consultancy in Namibia. She worked in a travel agency and was on her way to visit a desert resort outside of Dubai.

Would she want to see us? She had given me her card.

Would it be an imposition to show up at her workplace?

If you meet someone in an airport and exchange addresses, does it really mean that you can act on it?

Meeting Luciana in the airport was a stroke of luck. I wanted to visit Puglia.

Would we be able to find her?

We set out to search for Aradeo Street, number 42. Inside the city walls or outside? By midday we learned it was outside. When we stood in front of what should have been 42 Aradeo Street, there was no travel agency. Hot and tired, we approached a nearby coffee bar attendant and showed him Luciana's card. He laughed.

"Aradeo is a small town about forty kilometers from here. It's in the province of Lecce."

Wrong turns, misread directions, misunderstood language. Maybe this is not a good idea. On the other hand, we've come this far.

The next day we drove to Aradeo, the town. More a village than a town, the road seemed to end at the main piazza where the travel agency was located. We peered into the front window and spotted Luciana sitting at her desk. Yes, it was she. Long, dark hair.

And even still the doubt: Should we go in?

What will she say?

What will I say?

We walked in the door. Luciana stood up, tall with striking black eyes.

"Surprise!" I said.

She smiled and threw her arms open. "You made it!"

Audrey says: *A good way to get to Salento is to take the train from Rome to the city of Lecce, the de facto capital of Salento. The train ride goes along the western part of Italy to just north of Naples, then turns inland toward the town of Foggia on the Adriatic Sea, and finally runs south along the eastern coast and back inland to Lecce, the end of the line. The fascinating changes of scenery during the six-hour trip help to underscore the uniqueness of the beautiful coastline and endless olive groves of Salento. Of course, much faster is the one-hour plane flight from Rome to Brindisi, where it is possible to pick up a pre-arranged rental car.*

Today, my Puglia journals sit on the table in front of me. Faded purple sprigs of dry thyme fall out of the pages onto my desk. The perfume is gone. A few leaves of wild sage crumble into dry flakes. Here at home in San Francisco, it is a cold and damp winter. Can I bring back the warmth of our first visit to Salento, at Torre Pinta, an inn just outside the Adriatic seaside town of Otranto, where we sat on a patio and listened to the pulsating buzz of daytime crickets? Torre Pinta. The bridal suite: dark wood, towering wardrobe, lace bedspread, gold-framed paintings and mirrors. I remember the morning after, eager for the cool air of dawn, we sat outside the room on a shaded patio and looked out to pine, fig, and olive trees, the Adriatic Sea a blue strip on the horizon. We had yet to swim in it.

My scribbled notes are Italian vocabulary words, language lesson rules, places to visit, and reminders: Visit Santa Caterina church—famous for frescoes; look for the Maria Corti novel—early history of Otranto; *salice* means "willow" but is also a regional white wine. Is it red, too? Where do the locals eat? What's the word for breakfast?

I remembered our first meal together on the dining terrace of Torre Pinta with new friend Luciana and her mother, Netta, when Carlo and his wife, Lucia, arrived. Carlo was Luciana's high school English teacher. Both Carlo and Lucia were English literature teachers at Italian high schools in Gallipoli. Everyone except Netta spoke some English. When David and I tried to speak Italian, we found it impossible to be spontaneous. Our friends, impatient with our halting Italian but quite proficient in their English, easily switched between the two languages, though, as the evening went on, the prevailing language became Italian. Early on they asked us many questions about American English versus British English.

"How do you say good-bye in American English?"

We laughed and replied, "*Ciao!*"

Beyond *grazie* (thank you), *per favore* (please), and *buono* (good), there seemed to be little we could say. We smiled and nodded a lot. But even listening and comprehending weren't that easy, not to mention our befuddlement when our friends broke into the local Salento dialect. All those Italian lessons seemed to have been a waste as we succumbed to linguistic fatigue.

But then whiffs of rosemary and wild thyme stirred up by the night breezes blew past us, and when we looked at the animated faces of our new friends, drank more wine, and listened to the music of their spoken Italian (in other words, forgot about trying to understand), we relaxed. When the food arrived, the real party began.

Our first Salento food adventure began with *antipasti*, lots of it: *peperonata* (roasted red and yellow peppers swimming in olive oil), *melanzane* (eggplant cooked in olive oil), zucchini (summer squash in olive oil), *olive* (small, black and dried olives, with pits), *bruschetta* (toasted bread with chopped tomatoes and olive oil on top), *lampascioni* (wild onions), *pittule* (fried dough), and artichokes and dried tomatoes—in olive oil, of course. The terrace looked out over olive trees, the source of the olive oil. Families handpick their own olives and have them made into olive oil, enough for one year when the crop is a good one. The evening was warm and the sky was pink for a long time. Swallows welled up in small groups and darted after flies in the air. The dishes kept coming.

Oh dear, so many.

Should we eat a bit of each?

Would we insult these new friends if we skipped some dishes or left food on our plates?

But everything is so good and we're hungry.

So we eat. Mouths full. No need to speak.

The warm summer evening stretched late into the night, and the steady stream of food was never-ending.

The *primi* (first course) dishes arrived: *orecchiette* pasta (little ears) with *cime di rapa* (broccoli rabe), *cannellini* (large white beans) in a red-orange sauce, meaty, lemony, and light; and pureed fava beans with olive oil drizzled on top. Then a dish of well-cooked *cicoria* (chicory) greens arrived at the table along with horsemeat stew. Carlo explained that horsemeat was a typical and special dish of the area. The horses were bred only for eating purposes, and the meat was available at special shops. The stew tasted like gamey beef. Our hosts waited and watched. What did we think? Did we like it? I remembered years ago, as Peace Corps volunteers in Peru, we had been served the brains of a cooked guinea pig as honored guests of our Peruvian neighbors. In comparison, the horsemeat was delicious and that's what I said.

Carlo says: *In Salento, the horse was once a means of transport and a companion to man. When its laborious life was over, the animal gave its last contribution to the family it had served: its meat, cooked in a terra-cotta dish with tomato sauce, olive oil, pepper, bay leaves, rosemary, sage, and parsley. Today in Italy, and especially in most Salento towns, the tradition continues. One can buy horsemeat in one of the many horsemeat butcheries. Look for a* macelleria equina.

When the green salad was offered after the main dish, to aid digestion (we were told), we all agreed to skip it. For us this was either a reprieve or a bad idea, since at eleven thirty at night, stuffed and exhausted, we could have used some digestive help, but our friends insisted it was time for desserts (yes, plural): a plate of watermelon slices and whole peaches, then lemon sorbet and lemon cake. Espresso (no worries about caffeine so late at night, apparently) followed and sweet liqueur that we must drink (we were told) in order to help digest our food. Finally our digestive help had arrived!

We emptied tiny glasses of the traditional summer *digestivo*, *limoncello* (digestive liqueur made from lemons), desperate by now for relief. We were thirsty, too. The small water glasses provided just a few sips, and where were the ice cubes? Where was the pitcher of water? Our Italian hosts were content with small sips of chardonnay and water while we self-consciously refilled our glasses from the mineral water bottle on the table. At one in the morning, the meal ended. We were hot, sweaty, mosquito-bitten, too full, tongue-tied, and thirsty. Our culinary baptism, Salento style, was over. But we were also happy. We had fallen by chance and bits of effort and good luck into the embrace of Italian hospitality. Even in the state of having too much, how could we not want more?

Audrey says: *Our favorite restaurant in Otranto is* **Il Ghiottone**, *located on Otranto's Lungomare facing the sandy public beach. We have come to know the family owners, who always make time to talk with us and welcome us back to Otranto. The food and service are good, the place is comfortable, and the "Susumaniello" wine (from a local red grape) is delicious. Il Ghiottone is always the first restaurant we go to when we return to Otranto and where we eat our final meal before heading back to Rome and the States.*
Info: www.ilghiottoneotranto.it

Another favorite where the owners have become as much friends as restaurateurs is **Il Castello**. *We are regulars and highly recommend it. Otranto is very small, and you can just ask anyone where to find either restaurant.*

LUCIA'S FRITTATA WITH ZUCCHINI, MUSSELS, AND MINT

Frittata di Lucia di zucchine, cozze e menta

Lucia grew up with this summertime recipe made especially for visiting family guests from the north. Her grandmother made it, then her mother, and now Lucia, who tells us she can make it with her eyes closed. Zucchini, a summer squash, is plentiful in Salento, as are mussels, cultivated in the Taranto Bay. The Taranto mussels are small and tasty. Our Prince Edward Island mussels are similar. This recipe serves 4 to 6 people.

Ingredients:
7 eggs
6 tbsp pecorino cheese, grated
7–8 medium-sized zucchini, sliced into ¼-inch rounds
¼ cup olive oil
3 lbs small-sized mussels, scrubbed clean and debearded
1 cup clam juice to steam the mussels in (¼ cup white wine optional)
1 small onion, chopped
½ cup Italian parsley, chopped
A few leaves of mint, chopped
Salt and pepper to taste

Preheat oven to 350 degrees Fahrenheit.

Steam the mussels in the clam juice (and wine, if desired) until they open. Remove the mussels from their shells and set aside both the mussels and the cooking liquid.

Sauté onion and zucchini pieces together in the olive oil until soft.

In a bowl, beat the eggs together with a whisk. Blend the mussel juice into the beaten eggs and add the grated pecorino cheese, parsley, and mint.

Add the shelled mussels and the zucchini and onion mixture to the beaten eggs. Mix gently.

Pour all into a 9 x 12 baking dish.

Bake for 30–40 minutes or until the top is lightly browned.

Serve warm.

GETTING PERSONAL

Some people say that Santa Maria di Leuca is the point of land on the Salentine Peninsula where the Adriatic Sea meets the Ionian. Scientists say the meeting place is farther north and east along the coast; nevertheless the myth persists. Notes in my journal revealed my thoughts: Which sea is saltier? Bluer? What happens when a turquoise sea meets a deep blue sea? Is there a dividing line between the two? Are the fish different? Which sea is cleaner? Deeper?

On this, our first trip to Salento, we departed Otranto on the Adriatic coast for the road south to Leuca, a twisty passage along steep cliffs interspersed with wind-bent pine trees clutching the land, walled terraces with rows of olive trees, and isolated stone cottages perching precariously above the sea. A narrow bridge crossed over a deep chasm with seawater surging against the rocky crags below.

A few miles beyond the bridge, a tall white tower rose needle-like, pointing to the heavens, announcing the end of the land, *finis terrae*. The town itself was strung along the coastline like a necklace: a port for large and small boats, old villas, a hotel or two, and a few commercial wooden platforms furnished with beach umbrellas and chairs perched atop jagged seaside rocks.

We established ourselves alongside the sea on one of the wooden platforms and listened to the waves lapping at the rocks beneath us. Africa lay to the south, Albania and Greece to the east, and Sicily far to the west. A rope ladder with wooden steps at the end of a wooden walkway descended into the sea. Nearby, Italians in bright bikinis perched on rocks like exotic birds. We paid for our deck privileges while they, in rubber shoes, crawled over rocks and slid into the water. We would come back with our own rubber shoes next time. Beneath the clear water, stone boulders covered with spiny sea urchins broke up the patches of the white sandy seabed. Behind us a Romanesque church stood against the skyline while to its right loomed a castle tower built by Normans obsessed with defense in the eleventh and twelfth centuries.

Audrey says: *Before you cross the **Ciolo Bridge** on the coast road leading south from Otranto to Santa Maria di Leuca, you must stop and park in the small parking lot, walk across the bridge, and take in the view of the deep chasm beneath you. In the summer you will see swimmers climbing on the rocks and diving into the water. If you feel adventurous, follow the path down to the water and jump in for a glorious swim.*

Audrey says: *Santa Maria di Leuca, the farthest point south on the peninsula, is a quiet town with a walkway lined with mansions, beaches, and rocky coves for swimming and sunning. In the hills above the town, you can wander by car on narrow paved roads or on foot amongst olive groves and ancient stone walls, never out of sight of stunning views of the sea. My favorite places in the area are:*

Agriturismo Serine: *Organic olive oil and other farm products are for sale at this farm stay. Visitors are permitted to wander among the many garden fields planted with produce and fruit trees in addition to the groves of hundred-year-old olive trees. The farmhouse is open for reservations for lunch and lodging.*
Info: www.agriturismoserine.it

Osteria Terra Masci: *Good seafood and pasta are served for lunch or dinner on an outdoor patio covered by shade vines.*
Info: www.hosteriaterramasci.it

Villa Stasi B&B: *This bed and breakfast has a garden and an upper terrace within walking distance to the beach; the corner room facing the sea is the best. It is owned by the same family that operates the Serine Farmhouse.*
Info: www.villastasi.it

At midday, people disappeared. It was a Friday afternoon, and we found ourselves alone on our small section of wooden deck. Aha! It was lunchtime. Without a family of our own to join, our thoughts strayed to our family in San Francisco. Our son, Sam, and his Honduran wife, Jaki, had left his work with the Catholic Relief Services in Nicaragua a few months earlier. Together with their five-year-old son, Daniel, they had moved in with us, taking over the third floor of our house in San Francisco. Our son, unemployed and with some savings, was intent on living and working in San Francisco in some capacity as an urban planner with an emphasis on environmental issues. Jaki, trained as a nurse in Honduras, was studying for the California nursing exam.

Audrey says: *Afternoon rest time is one of the best traditions of Salento. Everything shuts down by 1 p.m. for lunch and quiet time. Urban areas open up again around 4 p.m. In smaller towns and the countryside, it's even later. In the summer, stores and restaurants stay open past midnight for late-night strolling and socializing, more often than not with a gelato ice cream in hand. Naps after lunch are necessary.*

We thought of our new Italian friend Luciana, close in age to our son, approaching forty and living at home with her mother, father, grandfather, and sister, Marinella. Luciana had graduated with a degree in education but was unable to find a teaching job. When we first met her, she was working for a travel agency. Early on, Luciana made it clear that working in the travel agency was not her chosen profession. One of the benefits of the job was to travel to new places in order to plan future tours for the company, which is how we met in Rome. Luciana said that in order for her to become a teacher she would have to interview for a volunteer position without pay and then hope that some kind of job would become available.

Her parents, Netta and Tullio, were both retired teachers. Marinella was also a teacher without a full-time job. She worked part-time as a Latin and Greek tutor. We could see how our son and his family, the same generation as Luciana and her sister, shared the same difficulties in finding work. Unlike the United States, it is normal for young Italians to be living at home with their parents. We felt less ill at ease in having our own son and family in our home, especially in tough economic times.

Carlo, Luciana's high school English teacher, and Lucia lived in the house where Carlo had grown up. His mother, now in her eighties, lived with them, along with their two boys, Davide and Matteo. In 2003, Matteo was studying engineering at the university in Lecce while Davide was still in high school. We met all of the family on an evening in July at the family summer house in Mancaversa, a follow-up invitation after our initial meeting for dinner at the Torre Pinta outside Otranto. We were excited about the opportunity to learn more about the area from people who lived and worked there. We hoped it would give us more opportunities to speak Italian. And so, on our first visit to the Mancaversa area, on the opposite side of the Salento Peninsula, Luciana arranged for us to stay at a summer apartment complex within walking distance of the Ionian Sea and our friends' summer homes.

Mancaversa

In Mancaversa, at the beginning of a short, dusty road to the sea, we found ourselves in a small white apartment with a kitchen, a bedroom, and a living area, complete with television and inside and outside tables. The patio had an outdoor shower, double sinks for washing clothes, and a large, multi-stringed clothes rack (an Italian *stendino*) with colored plastic clothespins. Another plus was the large outdoor shower with hot and cold water and privacy. Surrounded by high walls, we had no view to the sea, but the enclosed area was filled with trees, grass, and paths connecting the parking area to each apartment. The place was popular with Italian families, each cottage a private space, cozy and safe. The white walls shut out the outside world.

Throughout our stay, I scribbled notes in my journal: Was this style of architecture just an extension of the walled villas, towns, and castles so prevalent in the area from the time when pirates sailed up and down the coast, attacking and pillaging wherever they landed?

Uh-oh, I worried at first; too closed in, claustrophobic, especially with the ocean a short walk away. But surprise, I felt protected and secure! No need to shut windows or doors, even at night. One could sit naked in the patio in the hot afternoon hours—drawing, reading, napping.

Elisa, a young woman, managed the place, and one afternoon she and her grandmother sat outside their two-storied home in the center of the complex. On my way for a swim at sunset, I walked outside the front gate to the rocky shore, stopped, and greeted them:

Me: *Buongiorno, come estan? Vado al mare per fare il bagno.*

Elisa: *Benissimo, ma mi sembra troppo freddo. C'è vento!*

Later, I thought to myself: *Freddo* is "cold," right? Did she really say she thinks it's too cold? And I think I asked "How are you?" in Spanish . . . but they were too polite to correct me. Hmmmm, but the Spanish occupied this area for a long time, so maybe people do say "*Come estan*"? And *vento* is "wind," correct? Sure, there's a breeze, but how would I say "The water is warm even when the wind is cold"? And wait, does one say "*buongiorno*" even in the late afternoon? Or should I have said "*buona sera*," for good evening? Oh dear, is "*fare il bagno*" what you say in Spanish or is that Italian for have a swim?

At the water's edge, I struggled, fearful of falling on the slippery rocks. Where were my rubber shoes? With eyes focused on the breaking waves, I fell into the water as it surged against the rocks and then made my way through more rocks just below the surface until I was well out into the sea. I couldn't imagine how I was going to get back on land but I managed—a surging wave, a frantic grasp of jagged rock, and finally an adrenaline-fueled leg stretch to solid land that left foaming seawater behind to crash against the low cliff.

In Mancaversa, Luciana and Netta were the first to invite us to dinner. It was agreed that Carlo and Lucia would host us a few days later, on our final evening in the area. Netta prided herself on her cooking.

Luciana, too. We were invited to come early so that Luciana could drive us to the city of Gallipoli, a few minutes away, where we could watch the sunset. Gallipoli, an ancient city founded by Greeks, is on an island connected by a bridge from the modern part of the city. It is not the Gallipoli of eastern Turkey, site of the famous World War I battle. As we drove north along the Ionian coast, the old city sprang up above the sea, aglow like a jewel in the late afternoon sunlight, easily earning its Greek name "beautiful city."

We followed the shoreline of rocks, sand, and tall grasses until we reached the high-rise apartments of the modern city aligning the coast like sentinels. In a few minutes we walked across the old bridge, past a castle, and along the encircling seawall of the old city until we found the perfect bar with a perfect view of the sea.

Gallipoli

We drank Crodino, an orange non-alcoholic apertif, both bitter and sweet, and listened as Luciana delivered a short history of Gallipoli: an early Greek city with an ancient castle to protect it from pirates and Turks. Then Luciana's cell phone rang.

"Where are you?" asked Netta. "The pasta's been put on to boil, and you have exactly eight minutes to get to the dinner table."

"Don't worry," said Luciana, "she is only teasing us. We don't overcook our pasta. Nevertheless, we must go."

At the summer house in Mancaversa, we hurried up the steps and entered the dining room. Luciana introduced us to Marinella and her father, Tullio. Tullio, white-haired and smiling, served us our first tastes of *ricci* (sea urchins) with crusty white bread. Just hours earlier, Luciana's brother, Mauro, had plucked them off the submerged rocks along the nearby shoreline. Tullio cut them open with a sharp knife right at the dinner table and scooped the orangey, translucent eggs onto a small slice of white, saltless bread. The orange cluster of small, soft eggs tasted of the sea. We realized that we were eating *uni*, that opaque, burnt-orange blob available in our local sushi bar in San Francisco. Why did this sea urchin taste so much more flavorful and exotic?

ricci (sea urchins)

More food appeared: cooked yellow and red peppers; a bowl of mussels steamed in olive oil and wine; crusty, toasted bread with fresh, chopped tomatoes on top; orecchiette pasta with tomato sauce; and a platter of horsemeat in tomato sauce. Dessert was a large bowl of watermelon and peaches served with Italian sparkling wine.

Again, by the end of dinner, it was past midnight! We were tired. We were so full. Was this a special meal? Did everyone eat like this every night? Was it only in summer? How would we ever thank our hosts? They hardly knew us . . . yet such warmth . . . such abundance. We felt very special.

Luciana's father was quiet and soft-spoken with a twinkle in his eye. It was he who, on a later trip, introduced us to the *cappero* (caper) plant with its delicate, airy, white and lavender-streaked flower petals. The plant is cultivated locally but also grows wild along the rocky Salento coast and in between the crevices of stone walls, both urban and rural. It produces large capers the size of fat peas, unlike the smaller Greece-grown capers that we find in our San Francisco stores.

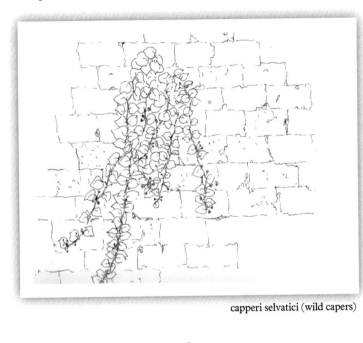

capperi selvatici (wild capers)

Netta was direct, casual, and friendly. She was curious about what we were talking about in English with her daughter.

"Have they been to Lecce yet?" she prodded. "Are you talking about the food? How long will they be here? Do they like it here?"

Marinella was smart and curious too but, like her mother, not an English speaker. Luciana stopped often to translate our conversation into Italian. Occasionally sparks of sisterly competition flew over this or that piece of information until one would cede reluctantly to the other.

"Our aunt did not graduate from grammar school," corrected Marinella at one point. "She went to a special school to learn sewing like all the other girls."

Luciana said something along the lines of it's not that important and asked Marinella to remove our digestivo glasses. Reluctantly, Marinella left the room.

Luciana was in charge, the daughter who had left home, lived in new places, learned English, and returned. Without her we never would have found ourselves at such a welcoming table.

On our final evening in the area, before we would board the train to return to Rome, we found ourselves at Lucia and Carlo's summer house for our good-bye dinner with Netta, Luciana, Marinella, and Elisa, the woman who ran the summer cottages where we were staying. We reminded ourselves that it would be a long evening of food and language, but now we knew what to expect. Our weak spoken Italian wouldn't hold out through the long night but eating and listening would. The summer house was barely a fifteen-minute walk away from our cottage and, just like Luciana's family's summer home, was large and beautiful, though a bit farther from the sea. The front courtyard had numerous plants and flowers. We ate on the open-air porch in the back of the house.

It was a hot and sultry evening. I sweltered in a long-sleeve linen shirt, clearly too warm for the occasion, while the other women looked fresh in simple sleeveless dresses. Remember for next time— dress for cool comfort. Servings of *antipasti* appeared. As the evening progressed, Lucia would bring a dish out from the kitchen, then Netta would disappear for a bit and emerge with another, and finally Luciana would bring out hers. Each would describe the food and sometimes question and argue a bit over its preparation: *fagiolini* (green beans), cooked peppers, eggplant, tomatoes and onions, prosciutto-covered melon balls, a quiche with mussels, a quiche with shrimp, a zucchini quiche, orecchiette pasta with broccoli rabe (frozen from winter), octopus with potatoes in a rich tomato sauce cooked in a *pignata* (clay pot) in the oven, olive bread (beware the pits!), small, round, pretzel-like crackers called *taralli*, sharp cheese made in the nearby university town of Lecce, Grana Padano cheese from the north, and finally dessert—watermelon, *pasticciotto* (cream pie), and almond paste candy in the shape of green and purple figs. And then, of course, Lucia's homemade limoncello. Late into the night, it remained humid and hot on the porch, no cooling breezes. As we continued to eat whatever came our way, tiny mosquitoes clung to my bare legs and enjoyed a feast of their own. Remember to bring bug spray.

We learned something very important that night that would serve us well on future visits and gatherings when food was served: one does *not* have to eat everything on one's plate. We were still getting used to the amount of home-cooked food at these late evening meals, and as each dish was carefully explained to us we felt that we should eat it all, out of respect for our friends, the cooks. But that evening we noticed that while they tasted the food they often did not finish it, excusing themselves by saying, for example, "Thank you but that's not my favorite food," or "I want to save room for the zucchini quiche, so I'll only sample the cooked peppers," or "The doctor says I shouldn't eat much pasta; it's delicious but I can eat only a bit of it," or "I'm allergic to seafood," or "You gave me too much but it's the best pasta I've ever tasted." On this first visit to Salento and our initial gatherings with friends, perhaps it would have been impolite to refuse the generous offerings of regional foods. But in future gatherings, as our friendship grew, we would use the language of our hosts and save ourselves from gluttony.

Late that evening, well after midnight, as we sipped our limoncello, Carlo played his guitar and sang for us. He presented us with two CDs of his music. We learned that in addition to teaching American literature at a Gallipoli high school he was a singer, songwriter, and guitar player in his own band, Bluesalento. But there was more. We were presented with a large coffee table book on Salento. Smiles and thank-yous all around, *abbracci* and *baci* to each cheek, and photographs and last-minute notes on the evening's recipes. We gathered our gifts.

What a reception!

What was the history of the area?

Why was it so easy to meet people and eat good food and swim in such clean seas?

And more challenging yet, how could we ever repay such kindness and hospitality?

Well, we tried. On our second visit to Salento, in mid-September this time, Lucia and Carlo offered us their Mancaversa summer home. School had begun, and they had moved back to their Taviano house. We had an idea: let's cook a Sunday dinner for everyone, something different, a Latin American/ Californian meal. We would give them a taste of our food but in their own country. Fish prepared with tomatoes and onions, Cuban black beans with rice, tortillas, and hot sauce, two kinds of melons, and vanilla gelato with rum and espresso.

On the day before our meal, we discovered that the old Gallipoli fish market had closed. It was moving to a new site. The thriving market we remembered with its bounty of fresh fish, shellfish, sea urchins, and sponges had disappeared. Not a good sign for our ambitious plan but too late to cancel. We were directed to a store with a freezer of frozen fish. We settled for a box (a whole box) of fifty small, frozen, frog-like fish. They would be good, a mild white fish, we were told. Maybe a fish lunch wasn't such a good idea? No, we can do this . . .

We found a grocery store just about to close at midday. How were we to know that some stores close midday on Saturday and don't open until Monday? We searched for black beans. We rushed about, befuddled by the huge packaging of goods until we realized that we were in a discount grocery with the regular grocery one level below; at last we found the beans, the rice, hot chili peppers, and tortillas, all imported goods.

Back in Lucia's tiny kitchen, the fish looked bony. The tomatoes weren't ripe. Tomato season was over. Maybe we should have bought a can of them. The garlic was in a package that upon closer inspection said "Imported from China." Oh dear.

We began our preparations that night: chopped the tomatoes and onions, put the black beans on to soak, made our own hot sauce, and worried mainly about the fish. What would it taste like? How bony? What about *antipasti*? None with this meal. Main dish first, American style. Well, maybe some local *taralli* with some prosecco. What if no one likes black beans? Too late to change now!

On Sunday, everyone arrived late. Just as we were about to cook the fish, the stove ran out of gas, thanks to hours of cooking the still-hard black beans. Luckily there was a tank of gas with the stove in a small kitchen in the back of the house. While David and I fussed with the food in the kitchen, Lucia set the table. We prepared each plate with rice, beans, and fish. The fish, like drowned frogs, struggled to emerge from beneath the tomatoes and onions. The hot sauce was tongue-numbing. The black beans, soft on the outside and hard in the middle, were too old for cooking. Burned-edge tortillas with soft, mushy centers. At the table, Italian politeness and American angst. Clear the plates, serve the melons! Luciana added bowls of grapes and plums from her garden. Finally the *fior di latte* (vanilla) gelato with rum and a dusting of espresso. It was over! Later, as we strolled along the Mancaversa beach promenade, our Italian friends showed us off: "Meet our friends, the *americani*."

the authors

We learned that we could never give back all that our Salento friends had given to us. How naïve to think that we could prepare a meal for such wonderful cooks! But we have found other ways of thanking our friends: making photo books of our visits together, treating them to dinners at new restaurants, writing down their recipes as they cook, and preparing and sharing their recipes when we are at home in San Francisco. We will always be guests at the receiving end of food, embraces, kisses, and gifts. We will eat too much, stay up too late, struggle to speak good Italian, and bask in that warm Salento womb. We will learn to accept our fate, gracefully.

PEPPERED MUSSELS

Impepata di cozze

Mussels are abundant in Salento. They are juicy, medium sized, and mostly cultivated in the sea waters near the city of Taranto, on the Ionian side of the peninsula. One of our favorite ways to eat them is as an antipasto. Salento mussels contain more juice than most, so we have found that when we prepare this recipe here in the States, we add some store-bought mussel or clam juice to the tomato mixture to create more liquid. This is an easy and delicious appetizer when served with bread fried in olive oil. Serves 4.

Ingredients:
2 lbs mussels, scrubbed clean and debearded
2 garlic cloves, finely chopped
15–20 cherry tomatoes, halved or quartered
½–1 cup mussel or clam juice (optional)
Fresh parsley, chopped
Olive oil
Black pepper, ground coarsely
Generous pinch of salt
4 slices rustic Italian bread

Add enough olive oil to cover the bottom of a large pot with a lid.

Add the tomatoes, garlic, the mussel or clam juice, a handful of chopped parsley, salt, and a generous portion of black pepper to the pot.

Cover and cook over medium heat for about 10 minutes or until the ingredients have released their flavors but not dried out.

Add the mussels.

Cover the pot once again and cook for 5 minutes over medium heat.

Remove the lid and shake the pot. Replace the cover and cook for 5 more minutes or until the mussels are well cooked and open. Set aside.

In a frying pan, add abundant olive oil to completely cover the bottom. Cut the 4 slices of bread in half and place them in the frying pan. Fry them in the olive oil over medium to high heat, turning as necessary until they are a toasty brown.

Pour the mussels and their sauce into a serving bowl. Place the toasted bread around the edges. Serve immediately!

SWIMMING IN BLUE SEAS

The first time we arrived in Salento we drove along the Ionian Sea on the eastern side of the peninsula on a warm and sunny day in June, too early for Italian beachgoers. School was still in session, no one on the beach, and hardly a car on the road. The water was blue-green, calm, and clear. My husband and I pulled alongside the dunes, stripped to our underwear, and dashed into the water—two rather out-of-shape sixty-year-olds but who was looking? A quarter mile away, the ancient Greek city of Gallipoli rose from the sea like a buoyant gemstone. Since that impromptu swim, we have returned every summer or fall to Italy, to the heel of the boot cradled between the Ionian and Adriatic Seas, to Salento. The province is Puglia but the tip of the peninsula, the region, is known as Salento. We love the people, the food, and the language, but it's that first glance of the sea that catches our breath and draws us into the sea, underwear and all.

Colors of the Salentine Coastline . . . we see them everywhere! We've visited one beach after another 7/14 - 7/15 . . .

Audrey says: *Salento's Gallipoli is a city on an island surrounded by the Ionian Sea, with a castle that dates back to the Byzantines. It has a swimming beach, baroque churches, restaurants, tourist shops, and a fish market and is connected to the modern city center by a small bridge. The Gallipoli castle is newly restored and open to the public. Walk around the island and stop for a drink, lunch, or dinner at one of the many outdoor restaurants with tables that look out to sea. My favorite is* **Trattoria Scoglio delle Sirene**. Info: www.scogliodellesirene.com

What is so magical about swimming off the coasts (Adriatic and Ionian) of Salento? Our Italian friends graciously tolerate our joyous ravings of swimming from sharp rocks or popular beaches. For them, the sea is too cold or too rough or the beaches are too crowded. They will swim only on a perfect day of warmth and sun and only in the late morning or late afternoon. But then, they get to choose when and where from late spring to autumn, while we are confined to our yearly visits.

One stormy morning in September, I approached the Mancaversa beach near the summer home of our Italian friends, teachers who had returned to work. We had their summer house near the Ionian seacoast all to ourselves. It was a stormy but sultry morning, and I decided to join my husband for a swim. A fisherman on the rocks shouted out to his fishing buddies, "Here comes the wife!" My husband was somewhere swimming in the open water, a transparent turquoise in summer but that morning a roiling blue-gray. The wind blew hard where I stood. The men watched. Would I go in? The waves breaking at my feet were warmer than the air. I took a deep breath and then another. Finally I crouched and slid forward into the waves. Sea salt stung my lips and burned my eyes. The waves, fierce and insistent on the surface, were surprisingly gentle and soft below. The fishermen returned to puttering with their fishing lines. The beach was empty. I'm sure they were thinking, "Only foreigners would swim in late September in a sirocco-wind-blown sea."

fishermen at Santa Caterina, near Gallipoli

fishermen on the *molo* in Otranto at dawn

Our Italian friend Luciana spent her summers at this beach as a child.

"It was a small cove and everyone was there every day," she told me. "No one learned to swim well, but everyone learned the basics from an older relative. Everyone kept an eye on the children. Nowadays, I hate to go there."

Otranto beach

She explained that all the kids she grew up with still come to the beach, though now they were married and had kids of their own—and although she was unmarried and childless, that was not what bothered her.

"It's the smallness of the beach," she said. "Everyone knows everyone's family history. What should be comforting is suffocating. There is always someone watching you."

I smiled and recalled the fisherman's "Here comes the wife." When I think of the roughness of the sea that day, I *appreciated* his watchfulness. If something had happened, I'd like to think that the fishermen would have offered a hand. But then, having grown up myself in a small town, I understood Luciana's discomfort and desire for anonymity. But, as I thought about it, it's the "if something had happened" that ties me to water.

As a child I took swim lessons at a local park, and one day I found myself out in deep water. I had followed an older girl who I desperately wanted to be friends with. She swam away from me and disappeared up a ladder while I bobbed up and down in water over my head. I remember flailing away until I reached the ladder and burst into tears. I don't remember if I was more upset at not being able to catch up with the older girl or overcome with the fear and elation of not drowning. Is fear (and overcoming it) part of the attraction of swimming? Perhaps, since I readily contend with the perils of tides, rip currents, jellyfish, submerged rocks, large waves, and boats.

Over the years, we have rented an apartment inside the castle walls of the small coastal town of Otranto. It lies on the Adriatic Sea side of the Salentine Peninsula and, as the most eastern city in Italy, is the first to celebrate the New Year. Almost every morning, before sunrise, we swim in the Otranto Bay. Often we are the first ones in the water, early enough to see the sunrise.

"Think of the magic and quiet of the sleeping town at dawn," my husband prompts. "Have your coffee later."

From bed to bathing suit, a grabbed towel and swim goggles in hand, down the stairs and out the apartment door, into the alley past Gigi and Rosaria's tourist gift shop, then past the Otranto Cathedral, its limestone façade glowing eerily in the pale light, we walk downhill, slapping the cobblestones with our flip-flops. At the bottom, trash collectors slam metal containers into a waiting truck. Forget the quiet dawn. Beyond the open piazza to the seawall walkway to the steep steps until we are level with the sea, then to the end of the cement pier where later in the day Italian housewives will settle in for sunbathing, gossip, and card games.

Audrey says: *Visit the* **Otranto Cathedral** *early in the morning before the large groups of Italian tourists arrive. Better yet, sit in on a wedding rehearsal or a Mass and listen to the organ music. Or, to observe Italian drama at its best, watch a wedding party as it enters or emerges from the church. The outfits are the latest styles. The wedding car is invariably an old or new luxury model. The brides are beautiful and poised as they make their way amidst flying rice and confetti, negotiating uneven cobblestones in dangerously high heels. Of course, the highlight of visiting the cathedral is its world-famous mosaic floor dating from the twelfth century with its trees of life motif, common in early Christian and Islamic art.*

Catedrale, Otranto
9-06

At the end of the pier, large boulders covered in sea moss fall into the sea and form crude and slippery steps unless it is late in June and the local card-playing Italian women have scrubbed off the sea moss with stiff brushes. We sit and shudder as waves break over our legs. We make final adjustments to our goggles and slide into the water, startling the fish nibbling on underwater rocks. We swim fast and steady until the shock wears off. I remember that once, halfway across the bay, a small, shiny circle in the sand down below caught my eye—a euro, well worth retrieving at the time, given the sinking value of the American dollar.

Otranto

We swim to the other side of the bay and back, easy to do when the water is calm. Heading back to the rocks, a few fishermen in small blue-and-white boats chug past us as they return from their early morning expeditions. On shore, two nuns wait to see what the fishermen will have to sell. We dry ourselves and take a minute or two to sit and listen to the spoken Italian, sometimes mixed with local dialect. People are polite. They manage to acknowledge our presence as strangers yet ignore us.

"*Buongiorno. Come va?*" Good morning. How are things?

"*Bene, bene. Tutto a posto.*" Good, good. Everything's fine.

After the greetings they look to each other and begin to clean the fish. Soon we are part of the scenery. We retrace our steps up the hill. With the first swim of the day over, it's time for cappuccino and pastries in the piazza, time to read the morning papers. This time, when we walk down the hill from our apartment, Gigi is opening his tourist shop and we exchange morning greetings.

Audrey says: *The seaside town of Otranto with its castle and cathedral is an Italian tourist destination. The alleys inside the walled city are filled with small tourist shops displaying ceramics, jewelry, clothing, toys, and linen weavings. Many of the shops are open year round. During warm summer nights the shops are open late. Luciana's mother, Netta, remembers visiting Otranto as a child, walking the alleys and buying small trinkets to take home.*

The doors of the cathedral are ajar, ready for the first tourists of the day. Early morning Mass is held in a side chapel on a lower level. As we pass the side chapel we glance in and see maybe eight to ten women in black, kneeling in prayer, and wonder why only women and why so few. We walk through the arched opening of the city walls and choose a café. Twenty or so feet away, beyond park benches, grass, and trees, the sea glitters. We choose a table close to Italians, usually men discussing politics or sports, so we can eavesdrop, perhaps pick up a local idiomatic phrase or two. The morning swim is forgotten as we dunk our Italian pastry into frothy cappuccino foam and struggle with Italian newspaper vocabulary.

Audrey says: *If you are going to stay three or more days in Salento, consider renting an apartment rather than staying in a hotel. Visit a rental agency or check online. On our second visit to Otranto, with the help of a local rental agency, we found an apartment with a terrace in the historic center and have returned to this same apartment every year. Our favorite rental agency is* **Derento Travel**. Info*:* http://www.derentotravel.com/derento/contatti.html

On the outside of the Otranto castle walls, fishermen keep their boats tied to the cement pier in the shallow water near the shore. Across from the boats is another cement pier where young children jump in. Older youth play rough games and shove each other off the wall into the water. If there are young girls in the area, the youths push each other more vigorously and shout and laugh as they show off. At the end of the pier where I usually sit I can look across the bay at the apartment buildings on the far side.

Audrey says: *The castle here is famous for its name, randomly picked off the map by Horace Walpole when he was writing his gothic novel* Castle of Otranto. *The castle was built by the Aragonese in the 1490s. It is now completely restored and used as a museum as well as an art and cultural center.*

Most summer days a group of Italian friends, mostly women, come to sit and play cards and talk about food and family. They are older women, fifty, sixty, and seventy, with bleached or dyed hair and deep tans. They wear the skimpiest of bikinis with aplomb and indifference to the rolls of leathery skin that gather between breasts and bellies. I often think that if they could be naked, they would. When I told my Italian friend Lucia that I admired the immodesty of these Italian sunbathers, she admitted that she had never worn a bikini. She believes that the bikini-clad overweight and older Italian women are behaving improperly.

"You may think it's liberating," she said, "but in my eyes, it's a breach of modesty."

I explain that the beauty for me is in the acceptance of aging bodies and being comfortable in one's own skin, but that won't change her mind.

the *molo* at Otranto

Just south of Otranto, within walking distance, is a beach and diving center called Orte. When we hike there, we take along our sunscreen and hats as protection from the relentless glare of sun on the open sea. In early June, the trails crisscross hillsides blanketed with blooming Queen Anne's lace, yellow daisies, purple thistles, red poppies, and clumps of rosemary, thyme, myrtle, and lavender. The air smells good. Just before we arrive at the wide, flat, and rocky cove, a shady pine forest softens the path with red pine needles. Beyond the deep shade and in between the slender, straight tree trunks, the early summer ocean sparkles. As the first swimmers of the season, we find no litter, no cigarette butts, and no umbrellas. The few flat rocks and sandy inlets are ours for the price of a chilly swim in pristine waters.

Audrey says: *It is possible to swim in warm water from May to October all along the coast of Salento, on both the Adriatic and Ionian sides of the peninsula. Bring along a pair of rubber or plastic swim shoes (jellies) when you come (or plan to buy one at any of the local beach shops). The shoes are often indispensable for negotiating the tufa rocks that line most of the coastline. Of course, there are* *sandy beaches here and there, but swim shoes are definitely an asset if you want to find less crowded areas. Indeed, beach shoes are standard wear among the Salentinians, who treat the rocky shoreline as if it were just another sandy beach.*

On the walk to Orte, we search for birds and find seedeaters, finches, larks, sparrows, and small hawks, or are they falcons? Our path crosses with that of a shepherd dressed in a white T-shirt and khaki overalls. He carries a small pack and is surrounded by shaggy, long-haired sheep and a few goats with large clanging bells beneath their chins. We pass the remains of a huge stone tower facing the sea, a relic from earlier times, now home to flocks of pigeons and the occasional rat looking for easy prey.

Hot and dusty, we arrive at the water's edge, fling off our clothes (we are the only swimmers), and enter the water by holding onto rocks and sliding our feet along the pebbles beneath the waves lapping the shore. The water is cold, and we are afraid of slipping and falling. Just when it reaches our knees, we squat and push off into the sea. It is not easy to do nor pretty to watch, this awkward, hesitant floundering. This is not the warm water of early September nor is it the serene bay waters of Otranto in July. But once we are submerged, we swim fast to warm up. Rock crevices open up to vast patches of white sand etched with the ripples of sea waves. Getting out of the water is as tricky as entering. Crawling works. Sometimes, giddy and unbalanced from the sun, sea, and swimming, it's best to fall back into the water, swim away from the shore, drift back in, and start all over again.

We walk back to Otranto along the same trail, but too quickly we are hot and thirsty and the cool swim is forgotten. Perhaps it was a good idea to walk through the flowering fields, but now the grasses scratch our legs and the sun scorches our skin. Why didn't we drive? But, of course, once we enter the town I will be the first to brag to our neighbors about the fabulous walk and the great swim, with no mention of heat, dryness, and the sun's incessant glare.

David says: *To get to the Orte swimming area by car, take the only road out of Otranto that passes the main market area and heads south along the coast toward the town of Santa Maria di Leuca. Turn left (via a roundabout) onto a dirt road at the "Orte" sign just outside of Otranto and follow the dirt road to its end. Park and walk south about a quarter mile on a well-worn path through the trees to the swim area. The view, the water, the snorkeling, and, if you're lucky, the solitude are well worth the effort.*

So why travel across the Atlantic and then south to the far side of Italy to swim? It's expensive and far. Our Italian friends say the sea historically has been something feared by those who live near it. But to us it's everywhere, available to all, and free of charge. Private beaches are few. Wherever there is open access to water, people swim. Jagged rocks cradle beach chairs and umbrellas and rubber-shoe-clad swimmers. People harvest sea urchins and octopus from rock crevices. The emerald and sapphire watery hues ebb and flow with the wind, sun, and floating clouds—a natural kaleidoscope. Beneath the surface, fish, rocks, sand, lost anchors, and abandoned pieces of rope move to the rhythm of waves. Swimming in Salento takes me back to the simple pleasures of youth. Where can you float, tread water, and swim so effortlessly but in a salty sea?

In the town of Castro, a few miles south of Otranto, early in the morning when all is quiet, I have watched elderly townsfolk arrive at the pier jutting into the sea. Before the sun rises, these older men and women slide off the rocks or climb slowly down the metal ladders attached to the cement sea wall into the cold, clear water. The silence is broken every now and then with a greeting, *buongiorno*, or a soft call for help into and out of the water, *jutame*. The swim strokes are slow and unsteady. After a few minutes, one by one, the swimmers leave the water, dry themselves, and return to their homes. I like to think that in their early morning swims they have captured a few moments of youth, freedom, and peace.

Antonio Verri, a Salento poet, says that the people of Salento are the color of the sea and walk with the rhythmic gait of a wave: *La gente, qui, ha il colore del mare, ha l'andatura di un'onda.* The color of the sea and the rhythm of the waves seduce and lull us into thinking that we foreigners, for a short time every year, can become the color of the sea and walk to the rhythm of a wave. But to be honest, there are days of swimming in Salento when the sirocco winds have churned up the waves so much that every stroke is a fight to breathe air and not gulp water. Waves may have a walk, a rhythm, but they also surprise and scare with currents and surges. There are days when a northern wind, a *tramontana*, has pulled icy cold water from the deep sea into the harbor, even in summer, forcing everyone to endure the cold or wade in shallow, warmer waters. At other times, the winds and currents may bring in tiny jellyfish, barely visible yet with a stinging bite, or large jellyfish known as *medusa*, easier to spot and avoid.

Back in my hometown park so long ago, having made it to the ladder on my own a second and third time, I reported to my teacher that I would no longer need lessons. I could swim. Years later, as a swim instructor at that same park, I used my own and my students' fears of the water to assure them that while the fears were real, they could be overcome, and that's what would make swimming even more joyful. Now, on the cusp of old age, my swims are shorter and less vigorous but still filled with the elation and the satisfaction of moving forward, weightless and free, swimming in the Adriatic or the Ionian Sea, red cap in place, goggles to protect my aging eyes, and the rubber shoes I have forgotten to remove.

Audrey says: *I like to bring small gifts home to my friends after a stay in Otranto. One of my favorite gifts for friends and myself is a bar of Salentum soap called "Salentissimo." The soap smells of flowers and the sea. There are Salentum stores in Otranto, Gallipoli, and Collepasso. Salento I profumi has its own Facebook page.*
Info: http://emiliasalentoeffettomoda.com/salentum-prodotti-e-profumi-salento/

IN LUCIANA'S GARDEN: HAVING A WONDERFUL TIME

Andiamo in brodo di giuggiole

The day was so windy that my husband and I skipped our morning swim in the Otranto bay and made arrangements to meet Luciana at her parent's house in Mancaversa, on the other side of the Salentine peninsula, where she was spending the summer. From there we would drive the short distance to the plot of land she had inherited from her grandfather. The distance between Luciana's family house in Taviano and the summer home in Mancaversa is only about five miles but the difference is great. Taviano is inland from the Ionian Sea. It is a typically dense Italian town of houses pressed close to each other on narrow, winding streets. Mancaversa is on the sea and its houses have verandas and gardens and space around them. Every summer, to escape the Taviano heat, the family makes numerous trips to Mancaversa as they cart clothes, kitchen gadgets, and food to the summer house. In between Taviano and Mancaversa lies a small plot of land enclosed by walls of stone and reached by a dirt road. This is Luciana's garden, a source of both pride and guilt.

Audrey says: *Many Salento families have two homes: a summer home on the Adriatic or Ionian coast and a winter home inland. Luciana and Carlo and Lucia live inland in the town of Taviano in the winter and move to Mancaversa, five miles away on the Ionian coast, for the summer months.*

Luciana's parents sit on the verandah that encircles the front of the Mancaversa summer house. Lucia and Carlo arrive as Luciana's father points out the damage to his porch plants caused by the strong morning wind. He calls it a *maestrale*, a summer sea breeze from the eastern Adriatic caused by the warmth of the land meeting the cool sea (although our Otrantini neighbors said the morning's wind was a *tramontana*, a wind from the mountains north of Trieste and Venice). In a few minutes, our Italian friends are arguing over the name and direction of the wind. Windy days are common in Salento, and the name of the wind depends on where it originates and where it arrives. Serious beachgoers will plan which side of the peninsula, the Adriatic or the Ionian, to visit depending on wind direction.

Meanwhile, we never learn if it is a maestrale or a tramontana because Luciana appears on the verandah and announces our departure to the countryside. We have joined Carlo and Lucia to go with Luciana for a visit to her garden. After so many years of friendship between Luciana, Carlo, and Lucia, this will nevertheless be the first time that Carlo and Lucia are seeing the garden.

Luciana wears a black dress with large yellow flowers and black shoes with a small heel. The lacy swirls of her Middle Eastern earrings swing back and forth as she previews our visit and explains that a spring hailstorm had destroyed a number of plants on the farm. In five minutes we arrive at the garden. Luciana tells us that she had been working this past school year in nearby Taviano, so she was able to come to the garden more frequently in the afternoons to water the plants and trees, unlike in past years when her teaching assignment had been too far away to allow her to care for the garden properly, causing her to feel great guilt as trees and plants succumbed to drought and neglect. On this visit, the garden shows her diligence. The water lines are all working and the trees are producing fruit. A large section of the land has been plowed for more planting.

"Someday, I want to build a summer house right there," Luciana says as she points to a white concrete shed. "My father is against it since there is a law that prohibits home building on agricultural property, though we both know that many people ignore the law. I want to build a prefabricated house made of wood, like your mountain cabins in the United States." She must be joking. There are no wooden houses in the region.

Lucia looks around at the fruit-laden trees and the stone walls that separate garden after neighbor's garden in all directions. "I hope you will include a hot tub when you build your house. We can sip wine and soak in the late afternoons after harvesting the fruit and vegetables!"

With the hot afternoon wind at our backs, we walk through the garden. Luciana explains that there are two kinds of almond trees, one bitter and one sweet. Lucia, Luciana, and I walk from tree to tree, testing the almonds. We pick numerous plum-size fruits, fuzz-covered and green, from the trees, then approach the nearest stone wall, where we place the fruit on a large stone and smash it with a smaller one. Next, we peel off the green outer skin and then the inner brown cover and finally take a bite of the whitish almond meat. Yes, this one is sweet, another is bitter. Sweet almonds are used to make almond paste for cakes and pastries.

"Oooooh, look at all the small snails on these almond trees," I exclaim, thinking that they must certainly be nasty parasites.

"The larger snails are picked off and taken home to be eaten," Luciana says, "and the smaller ones are scrubbed off the tree trunk; that is, if one has the time and energy. The snails are pests that eat the green leaves and the flowers of the tree. They can destroy it if they are not kept in check." She adds that although there is a powder that can be put at the base of the tree to discourage the snails, she has never used it.

As we walk around the property, I gather the conversations on a small tape recorder so that I can learn the Italian vocabulary. Lucia, impressed by Luciana's botanical knowledge and expertise, exclaims "*caspita*" at every plant and tree, the equivalent of "oh my gosh," "goodness," or "you don't say!" Carlo tells me about a tree called "*giuggiolo*" that produces date-like fruit called "*giuggiole*." He explains that there is a saying in Italian: "*andare in brodo di giuggiole*," which translates literally to "walk in the juice of the giuggiole fruit" but idiomatically means to enjoy something very much, to be very pleased by something, to be thrilled, to be enraptured. Luciana, unintentionally shedding more light on her grandfather, comments that he hated giuggiole. I try out the new Italian idiom by announcing that at this very moment, we are *andando in brodo di giuggiole.*

The freshly irrigated soil in Luciana's garden is a deep red, iron-rich mud. It invites handling that brings back memories of childhood mud cakes perfect for playtime lunches. We bend down and yank out wet weeds. The mud soaks into the cracks of our hands and burrows beneath each nail and then dries to a crust. David works the most conscientiously pulling out weeds. I stop after Luciana points out that I have just pulled out a young eggplant seedling. The tomato plants are easier to recognize so I move on, but when I run into numerous nettle plants intertwined with other weeds I decide it's time to head to the irrigation barrel with its cool water dripping from a hose draped on an olive tree branch. Luciana mentions that all the irrigation tubing is marked with the family name so that it will not be stolen, though theft remains a problem.

We congregate near the white shed she had pointed to earlier. Lucia is afraid of the gecko families that lounge on the rafters and walls yet dart unexpectedly when disturbed by light and noise. She refuses to enter the shed. It is freshly whitewashed, and the window frame and door are painted a royal blue. Inside it is cool and dark. Our voices echo in the space. Old farm implements hang from the wall. Someone picks up a pitchfork and says, "This would be great for catching an octopus." We laugh. Back outside, the hot wind blows and the argument over the wind begins again. Is it a tramontana or a sirocco? Luciana tells us her father is making her put in a new metal door and metal shutters to make the shed more secure. She prefers the ancient wooden door and shutters but admits that theft of fruits and vegetables along with equipment is becoming more frequent.

By now, we are hot and dry. My sandals are heavy with mud. Luciana's black heels are crusted with a thick layer of it. Lucia holds a bag brimming with lemons. Carlo begins to list the trees in *his* garden, located in his backyard in Taviano. The wind blows hot on our faces, but no one has the energy or interest to discuss where it is coming from or what it is called. It is time to call it a day.

Later, at home in San Francisco, I listen to the voices on the tape recorder from our afternoon "*in brodo di giuggiole.*" In the background I hear the wind gusting into the microphone. Yet the spoken words of our Italian friends have been recorded and are poetry:

Guarda la menta! Pura menta!   Look at the mint! Pure mint!
Vera menta!   Real mint!
E' mentuccia!   Large leaf mint!
Si chiama menta spicata.   It's called spearmint.
Non la piperita.   Not peppermint.
Questa é la menta selvatica,   This is the wild mint,
profumata, quasi piccante.   perfumed, almost spicy.

Prendine quanta ne vuoi!   Take as much as you want!
Siamo contadini a riposo.   We are farmers taking a break.
Questi sono fichi.   These are figs.
Queste sono melegrane.   These are pomegranates.
Queste sono mele selvatiche.   These are wild apples.
Fichi e fichi d'India   Figs and prickly pears
La susina, la prugna   Plum, prune
Quanto mi piace!   I love it so much!

Il vecchio pero.   The ancient pear tree.
L' anno scorso ne abbiamo mangiate molte.   Last year we ate so many.
Buona, buona!   So good, so good!
La mia uva, appena piantata.   My grapes, just planted.
Un bellissimo nocciolo.   A beautiful hazel nut tree.

Il nespolo, il limone.	The loquat tree, the lemon.
Cesti, sacchetti, sacco	Baskets, small bags, a big bag
Zanzare, gechi, alberi	Mosquitoes, geckos, trees

Luciana says: *Of course, my garden is a family treasure, but if you are interested in seeing a true botanical garden that has collected plants from all over Salento and the world, visit* **La Cutura Botanical Garden,** *located in the Palmariggi-Giuggianello area about a half hour south from Lecce. This fabulous botanical garden offers every imaginable garden style. Its stunning greenhouses contain the largest array of cacti to be found in Salento. There are also lots of other small sections devoted to a variety of plants: a rose garden, an herbal garden, a classic Italian-style garden, a Mediterranean garden with a forest of evergreen oaks, and even a rock garden and a secret garden.*
Info: http://www.lacutura.it/

PIZZA WITH VALENTINA AND PIPPI

It was a Monday afternoon in the middle of summer in Salento when my husband and I along with our Italian friends Carlo and Lucia arrived at the summer home of Pippi (short for Giuseppe) and his wife, Valentina, for a light supper of homemade pizza baked in a backyard brick oven. Carlo and Pippi had grown up together during summers in Mancaversa by the sea. Pippi and Valentina were in their late fifties and worked together in an accounting firm they had begun many years before in the inland town of Taviano, three miles away, where they had their "winter" home. They had raised three children who were now on their own, one in Australia, one in Brussels, and a daughter, about to give birth, living in Mantua in north-central Italy.

Pippi was an expert at catching octopus, and he was prepared to answer our questions about how it was done. We had heard that fishermen who plied their trade along the Salentine coast caught each octopus individually, and yet it was difficult for us to imagine that they were all caught one by one. Was it true? Carlo assured us that Pippi would be able to answer all of our questions.

Octopuses are plentiful in Salento and are often cooked in their own juices in a clay pot or served with parsley and lemon in a salad. Pippi confirmed that octopuses were caught individually and launched into an explanation of how he catches them by using a multi-pronged hook with a dangling black spider made of rubber and a large weight that anchors the line at the bottom of the sea. Imagine an octopus hidden in the rocks when suddenly a jiggling black spider appears before it. The octopus darts out from its lair, wraps its tentacles tightly about the spider, and finds itself entangled on the hooks. Pippi showed us all of his homemade hooks and lures and explained that Salentine fishermen take pride in their unique handmade octopus lures.

Pippi's octopus lure

Maybe it was all the talk about octopus but I was beginning to get hungry. An hour or so had gone by and I wondered, What about the pizza? The kitchen off the back deck was quiet, and Valentina was nowhere to be seen. And where was the famous outdoor oven?

My measure of the best pizza came from years of eating at Verdilini's, a Neopolitan family restaurant that closed its doors long ago, in Meriden, Connecticut. Pizzas were served on long rectangular sheets with not too much sauce or cheese and crusts that were always perfect, not too thick or dry but with a melt-in-your-mouth chewiness and a mild sweetness—the kind of crust that we would take home and eat cold for breakfast with coffee the next morning.

In our own search to imitate that perfect pizza, my husband had experimented at our home in San Francisco. We bought a pizza stone to make the oven as hot as possible, and while the pizzas were delicious, the oven was never hot enough to make that perfect crust. We had even considered building our own brick pizza oven in our urban backyard.

But no mention of pizza yet that summer afternoon in Salento.

Next, Pippi guided us to the new swimming pool with its two large boulders unearthed during excavation. He explained, "The boulders in the pool were found when we excavated the earth for the pool. It seemed right that they went back into the pool when it was finished."

The milky, tan-colored stone masses, large enough to break the water's surface, glowed in the late afternoon sun. Frogs jumped from the edge of the pool to the boulders, capturing both the light and the mosquitoes that danced on the surface. Beyond the pool were native trees, herb and flower gardens, and beehives.

"What's this?" Pippi asked as he pointed to a bunch of Italian parsley.

In Italian, I answered, "*Prezzemolo.*"

"*Bravissima!*" he replied.

A pedestal in the middle of the yard, not far from a water lily and goldfish pond, supported a large sundial designed by Pippi, who continued to test my Italian vocabulary.

"What's this?"

"*Menta.*" Mint.

"And this?"

"*Basilica.*"

"*Basilico,*" he corrected. Basil, not a large building, as in Saint Peter's Basilica in the Vatican.

"Ah, *sì, basilico.*"

"And this one?"

"*Timo.*" Thyme.

Meanwhile, Valentina appeared and, unwilling to be left out of the guessing game, ran into the house and emerged with a small bowl she stuck under my nose.

"Smell this," she said.

A deep, rich, and yeasty perfume rose from a small, light yellow pillow of dough made from flour mixed with water.

"Yeast," I said.

Valentina replied, "Enough flour and water until it feels like elastic and holds together . . ."

"Yes, the yeast . . . those little packages of yeast from the grocery store," I said.

"No, no yeast. Magic! I don't buy yeast. I cover a bowl with a cotton napkin and place it beneath the trees in the yard for one to two days. The bowl collects the bacteria in the air and turns the mixture into a natural yeast."

I had never heard of this before. What was the science behind it? Would it work in our backyard at home in San Francisco? I would have to remember this, although the chance of finding clean city air with healthy bacteria floating in it seemed pretty slim.

We were getting hungry and it was getting late, yet no one paid much attention to the small brick outdoor oven sitting rather forlornly at the end of the yard behind the house. It didn't look as if a pizza dinner would be underway any time soon. Another late night. Would I ever get used to long summer evenings? At least the yeast was ready and waiting!

As we wandered away from the swimming pool area, Pippi began to gather stray branches, leaves, and pine cones lying about the yard, saying, "One of the good things about getting the pizza oven ready is that it provides an opportunity to clean up the yard."

I looked at the expansive yard. Hmm, there will be pizza after all, but it will take a bit of time. Pippi enlisted Carlo, my husband, and me in the gathering of multiple armloads of yard debris and making a growing pile alongside the pizza oven. The dry vegetation would be used for the initial warming of the oven. When just the right amount of kindling had been assembled, he lit the fire. We continued to add to the pile and watched as Pippi tossed a mix of trimmings inside and used a long wooden pole to shove them back into a small shrine-like space. Little by little he added more material. It burned hotter and hotter. After about an hour of feeding the wood trimmings and pine cones and finally small logs to the fire to make the walls of the oven turn white with heat, the oven was ready for the pizza. We stood peering into the furnace and felt the heat on our faces. Meanwhile, in the kitchen off the terrace, Valentina was running behind schedule.

Pippi shouted, "The oven is getting hot! Make the pizzas!"

Valentina ignored him. She was on the phone with her pregnant daughter in Mantua. The discussion appeared serious and unending. On the kitchen table sat a wooden board sprinkled with yellow semolina flour. On top of that was a small volcano of regular flour mixed with a bit of the grainy semolina, which looked like stone-ground cornmeal.

Pippi shouted louder this time. "The fire's almost ready! Where's the pizza?"

Valentina shouted back, "I'm on the phone, can't you see?"

Lucia, Carlo's wife, stepped up to the table and began to mix the dough, but Valentina interrupted her, saying, "Wait." Lucia grabbed some dishes and silverware and headed for the table outside on the deck. I grabbed my camera and left the kitchen quickly, the heat of the oven and the frantic Pippi preferable to the tension in the kitchen.

Pippi swept the hot oven floor with branches from the aromatic *mirto* (myrtle) bush, pushing the cinders off to the side. "Cleaning the oven floor," he explained, "to make an aromatic bed for baking the pizza." He closed the oven's heavy iron door.

Valentina was still talking on the phone, holding it with a raised shoulder while her hands mixed the dough.

Pippi, throwing up his arms in frustration, yelled again, "It's ready! Where's the pizza?"

"It's coming," yelled Valentina, who had finally gotten off the phone. Oh good, at last I could return to the kitchen. I watched Valentina dart to the refrigerator and fill her arms with a jar of homemade sauce, sausage, local green olives with pits, cooked eggplant, and mozzarella cheese.

Pippi, worried that the fire had lost its perfect level of heat, shook his head in defeat. "It may be too late."

Valentina spread the toppings quickly onto stretched dough, which was threatening to come apart. "This will have to do, holes and all." She rushed through a beaded curtain, out to the deck, and down the stairs, the most difficult part still ahead.

Pippi opened the oven door and shook his head. "It may be too late."

"No," insisted Valentina, "it will be fine."

Together, he and Valentina nudged the pizza off the wooden paddle into the depths of the oven, still white with heat. For a moment the pizza stuck to the board and almost stretched apart into two pieces.

Pippi shouted, "It's too late!"

Valentina concentrated on shaking the long-handled board so that the pieces of dough jammed together. It would not be a perfect exchange from paddle to oven floor this time.

Pippi shut the door, smiled, and shrugged his shoulders. "What's done is done." Maybe it was always like this . . . mounting tension, shouting, and a dread that the pizza would never leave the wooden paddle.

Three minutes later, the pizza was ready!

A large, modern, florescent light illuminated the deck and yard. Valentina announced that she only drank beer with pizza. We would, too. We clicked our glasses together in a toast to our hosts. How many hours had gone by? It was dark and the stars were out. We spooned homemade *caponata* made of diced eggplant, summer squash, and tomatoes on top of our pizza slices. The pizza was delicious. The crust was superb. We were sated. It was getting late. We remembered that Carlo and Lucia had promised that it would be a pizza-only meal, perhaps with melon for dessert. Then Valentina disappeared into the kitchen and quickly returned with a large bowl of potato salad in one hand and a large plate of long green skinny beans called *fagiolini* in the other. Behind her, the beaded curtain jangled as if mocking our thoughts. We were fooled yet again into thinking that this would be a simple meal of pizza!

Pippi explained how he had prepared the *fagiolini* with sea salt, red wine vinegar, and olive oil. Later came the watermelon, cut into large chunks, then Lucia's orange cake followed by sweet homemade watermelon sorbet. Near midnight, we sipped tiny glasses of *mirto* (liqueur made with myrtle berries) and limoncello as Pippi regaled us with stories about his ocean-diving days and his extensive shell collection.

What an evening! As we walked to our car, we stopped once more by the pool for another look at the delirious frogs, jumping with abandon from boulder to boulder like young boys on the rocks that line the Salento seacoast.

On the drive back to our apartment, we wondered out loud, "What about that idea of building a pizza oven in our urban backyard?" Gather the branches, build the fire twig by twig, sweep clean the oven floor, slide the pizza into the oven at precisely the high-heat moment, watch out for elbows, don't let the dough stick to the wooden paddle, take it out in time! We looked at each other and laughed. "Not a chance!"

We knew without saying that from now on, the gold standard of pizza rested with Pippi and Valentina in the backyard of their summer house by the sea in Mancaversa, Salento, Italy. As we reflected the next day, the ingredients of that perfect pizza were more than dough and sauce—they were the anticipation, hunger, drama, tension, the magical organic yeast, the golden semolina, the sauce from sweet homegrown tomatoes, the friendly sharing, the music of the Italian language, even the croaking of the frogs in the pool.

Audrey says: *When we can't have Valentina and Pippi's homemade pizza, the next best pizza in all of Salento is that made by the* **Ristorante Pizzeria Bella Napoli**, *located in Torre Suda-Racale along the Ionian Sea, on the Via Lungomare. It is just down the road from Luciana's and Carlo's summer homes in Mancaversa. Families sit at long tables in the center of the room while tables for two line windows looking out to rocks and the sea. An outside terrace has more tables. Pizzas are ordered by the meter and are placed on holders about ten inches above the table top like offerings to the gods. The crust is thin, crispy, and slightly burned around the edges. The Bella Napoli pizzas are balanced in the proportion of toppings to crust. No Americanized overload of cheese or meat!*

Info: www.bellanapolitorresuda.it

VALENTINA'S PIZZA

Pizza da Valentina

Although Valentina swears by her "magical yeast," the following recipe suggests that you use a packet of "wild" yeast from your local food store.

Preheat the oven to 550 degrees Fahrenheit: If your oven can be set higher, use the highest setting. If possible, use a pizza stone and preheat the oven for at least 30–45 minutes with the pizza stone in place on a rack just above the center.

Ingredients for the dough:
½ cup warm water
2¼ tsp yeast ("wild" yeast, if available)
3½ cups bread flour
1 tsp salt

Add the warm water to a large bowl and sprinkle the yeast on top of it. Let it sit until the yeast is dissolved (about five minutes). If needed, stir to dissolve completely.

Mix in the flour and salt.

Knead by hand until the dough is smooth and elastic.

If the dough seems a little too wet, sprinkle in a bit more flour.

Place the dough in an olive oil-greased bowl and cover with plastic wrap. Let sit in a warm place until it doubles in size, about 1 to 1½ hours.

While the dough is rising, prepare the pizza sauce and toppings as below.

After the dough has risen, work it briefly, flattening it with your hands on a lightly floured work surface. Start at the center and work outwards, using your fingertips and palm to flatten the dough out to the edge until it is about a ½-inch thick. As you are flattening the dough, you can sprinkle flour on the top side and flip the dough so it doesn't stick. When you are satisfied that the dough is thin enough and of more or less even thickness, you can pinch the very edges if you wish to form a lip.

Preparing the Sauce and Toppings:

Ingredients:
¼ cup olive oil
½ cup fresh tomatoes, chopped (or your favorite pizza sauce)
½ cup fresh basil, chopped
½ cup fresh mozzarella cheese
Grated Parmesan cheese

Possible additional toppings:
Mushrooms, thinly sliced
Onions, thinly sliced
Italian sausage, cooked ahead
Prosciutto, pepperoni, or similar
Whatever other topping your imagination suggests

To ready the pizza for the oven, sprinkle a liberal amount of flour on a wooden pizza paddle and transfer the flattened pizza dough onto the paddle. While loading the sauce and toppings, give the paddle an occasional shake so that the pizza dough doesn't stick when ready to put into the hot oven.

Working quickly to keep the dough from sticking to the paddle, drizzle a small amount of olive oil onto the dough and spread it around with your fingertips. Sprinkle a light layer of Parmesan cheese. Spread the fresh chopped tomatoes or tomato sauce on the pizza dough. Sprinkle on the chopped basil. Spread the remaining toppings and mozzarella cheese. Sprinkle another light layer of Parmesan over all.

Don't load up your pizza with too many toppings as the baked crust will fail to crisp like it should on the hot pizza stone. Also, too much meat of any kind is unnecessary and more typical of the American distortion of a true Italian pizza. Use just enough meat topping to allow an occasional taste of the flavor while not overpowering the delicate flavor of fresh tomatoes, herbs, and cheese.

Slide the pizza off of the wooden board onto a pre-heated pizza stone into a very hot oven.

Bake the pizza about 7 to 15 minutes until the crust is browned with the edges slightly charred. The hotter your oven, the quicker your pizza will cook.

CHAPTER TWO

Luciana

THE RACONTEUR

I was born and raised in Salento and still spend most of my time there. Like most Salentinians, and most southern Italians in general, I have always had a conflicted relationship with my hometown and with my native land. I am Salento's harshest critic while I am here, yet I am fiercely defensive when outsiders speak ill of it.

I left Salento at the age of eighteen, headed to Tuscany, the cradle of Italian Renaissance, home to

Dante, Michelangelo, Leonardo, Galileo, to the finest culture, art, literature, to the purest expression of the Italian language. What I left behind seemed, at that time, of so little importance. What was Salento, after all? Nothing more than any other backward southern province forgotten by men and gods?

I never met so many Salentinians as when I was in Pisa at the university. We didn't tend to form "ethnic clans" like the Calabrese or Sardinian students. Still, the Salentinians were well visible, made fun of because of our insistence in defining ourselves as Salentinians and not by that meaningless geographic adjective "Pugliese." Meeting away from home was always occasion for long disquisitions about how we missed our *frise* (toasted bread covered with sweet cherry tomatoes) and whether the turquoise Ionian Sea with its sandy beaches or the cobalt Adriatic Sea with its rocky coast and caves was to be awarded a prize for the best spot in the world. All of the endless homesick arguing and chanting was strictly in dialect. It was in Pisa that I learned to speak the *Salentu* dialect. In Pisa I heard and danced my first *pizzica*, a Salento folk dance, or at least the first time I felt it was "mine."

The Salentine reunions in Pisa often ended over a plateful of *ciceri e tria*, a Salento chickpea and pasta dish, and a glass of Salice Salentino, a treasured local wine. Our families cared for us, sending all sorts of goodies on a monthly basis as if we were in a savage land and we couldn't survive without the taste of our local food. We actually could hardly do without it. The longing for Salento grew bigger and more anguished with time. Cycling in one of the most luscious regions of Europe, gifted by God with gentle hills covered in green and crossed by slow, majestic rivers, I nevertheless felt my heart beating for that faraway tip of land that hadn't changed the world or given us the Renaissance, that couldn't even boast a Florence or a Siena. Salento has always been at the end of the line, no more than a poor, rural relative of Tuscany; a sun-drenched heel of the Italian boot with its dusty roads flanked by gnarled olive groves and its gleaming white *masserie* (old farmhouses). But in its little white villages, time runs at a different pace—a pace that makes the quality of life unparalleled.

Every train journey home for the holidays was a trip toward my soul. Year after year, trains became more and more crowded with mostly Italian tourists heading to Salento. Now that I had recovered my love for that land, I began to wonder what these "strangers" were looking for. What was attracting them to Salento? Was it some tourist brochure advertising its inordinately large and varied coastline, still waiting to be developed? Was it the southern climate that invites year-round tourism? The call of the baroque? The magic of *trulli*, cone-shaped houses attached to one another? What did these visitors expect to find in Salento, and what would they remember upon their return home?

In the past, many tourists were familiar with Puglia's *trulli* and its large coastal city, Bari. They had to cross the area on their way to the ferries destined for Greece. Yet few ventured farther south. I began to promote the richness of my Salento, with its southern Italian history and intriguing mix of traditions: the remains of Greek and Roman temples; prehistoric monuments scattered amidst cacti, olive groves, and abandoned tobacco farms; Gallipoli's Arabic-influenced architecture; Greek-speaking villages around Castrignano dei Greci; and Giurdignano's prehistoric *menhir*, a stone monument looming over a Byzantine crypt.

I saw and appreciated, as if for the first time, our historic Italian towns: Lecce, the Florence of the South, with Zingarello's baroque-carved churches, a university, and a Roman amphitheater; Gallipoli, with its old town and a restored castle on an island bridge; Otranto, on the Adriatic coast, with its eleventh-century cathedral; and Galatina's Saint Catherine's church, with its Bible-story frescoes "tattooed" on the walls and pillars of its interior.

Luciana says: *The frescoed interior of the* **Basilica di Santa Caterina d'Alessandria** *in Galatina makes it one of the most interesting churches to visit in Salento. Glorious frescoes depicting stories from the Old and New Testament cover the walls and pillars from floor to ceiling. Make sure to check the times that the church is open for visitors.*
Info: http://www.basilicaorsiniana.it/

Still, I insisted in denying this motherly or daughterly love for Salento. I had learned where the beauty was but still had more to learn about the soul of the place. I insisted on the intolerable insularity of the place. When you are on vacation here, I said to myself, it's easy to adjust to the rhythm and let the practicalities of life (like work) drop to the wayside. But living here is different. It took me more years to move from the "I couldn't live here" to the "I couldn't live elsewhere."

So I completed my studies in Pisa and was able to spend a year in London, studying English and preparing for a career as a teacher. If you ask why I chose a teaching career, the answer also has its roots in Salento and its traditions, which, of course, had influenced the lives of my parents.

My parents, my sister, and I have all become teachers. My mother and father both taught the United States' equivalent of elementary school. On the pages of my town's telephone directory, my home number is listed under my father's name, Tullio Cacciatore, in the following way: "Cacciatore MAESTRO, Tullio." *Maestro*. Not simply "teacher," but "master," which connotes a higher level. It implies example, rectitude, paramount skill, model, reverence.

That's how schoolteachers have historically been addressed in Salento; maestro is a lifelong title. The teacher has been seen as a model to be emulated. Sometimes he or she was viewed almost as a mythological figure. Your teacher took you by your hand at the age of six and brought you through the forest of words, lines, alphabets, syllables, dictations, spelling mistakes, multiplication tables, the twenty regions of Italy and their provinces, memorization of patriotic and inspirational poems, monthly tales from the book *Cuore* (Heart), Garibaldi and his wounded leg, bruised knees, and lame excuses for homework not done.

Luciana says: *Most Italian school children have read the novel* Cuore *(Heart), written by Edmondo De Amicis at the time of Italy's unification in 1886. It is a children's novel constructed as the scholastic diary of Enrico, a ten-year-old primary school student in Italy with an upper-class background who is surrounded by classmates of working-class origin. The entire chronological setting corresponds to the third-grade year, with topics that revolve around moral values: study, work, respect for order and hierarchy, dignity, honor, helping those in need, love for family and friends, sacrifice, and patriotism. It is a good book to read for the flavor of the times, but today, many Italians dismiss it as cheesy and dislike its rather pathetic-sentimental key.*

Being a teacher granted a status, a few steps lower than the priest and almost on a par with the village doctor or pharmacist. These teachers, my mother and father included, often knew their students better than they knew themselves. They knew families, situations, circumstances. And families looked up to teachers as those who would be entrusted with the education of their children—a task that implied something larger than good spelling and mathematics, much more than mere knowledge.

Still, you may ask what has brought me to undertake this career? It is too easy to say that it is because my parents were both teachers. I do not doubt that what brought me to undertake the teaching career was my father's immense respect for his own education.

My father's father, Cosimo, was a *contadino*, a peasant farmer. Indeed, among my acquaintances, it seems that nearly everybody's grandparents were peasants. My father had to struggle to get the education that ultimately enabled him to become Maestro Cacciatore. He was the third of four children. My grandfather recognized his role as breadwinner, and at that time, the breadwinner was invariably a peasant who worked the land. He had a stern, old-fashioned sense of honor. His wife and daughters could not be seen working in the fields. It would have diminished his image. He would have preferred to multiply his efforts, doing many jobs to make the ends meet, as long as his women could stay safely at home. Unfortunately, Grandfather's meager earnings meant that only the eldest son, my uncle, was allowed to get an education. This was enough of a drain on the family's savings that they could not afford to pay for the education of their younger son, my father. Moreover, my father's work and presence in the home were needed.

My father knew it was not an injustice to be denied an education. There just wasn't enough money. Yet I can only conclude that the family's limited resources increased my father's resolve to get his own education. So, although it was much later, my father completed his studies, supporting himself by engaging in the most difficult and toughest menial jobs, such as carrying stones and working twelve-hour days as a peasant in the sun-baked fields of others. His memories of family life never fail to summon pictures of those hardships. And yet, above all, my father had the highest regard for his education and his finally achieved position as a maestro.

And so I, too, now proudly say that I am a teacher and that I am a Salentinian.

GRANDFATHER COSIMO

Cosimo, my father's father, was a man of the early twentieth century. He fought in World War I, as did thousands of other peasant soldiers, on mountains whose names he could not even pronounce properly. I doubt that these soldiers, summoned from their remote areas by this otherwise unknown entity called Italy, had any notion of the reasons, the rights and wrongs, of that war. All they knew were the usual lies that peasants were told: at the end of the war there will be more wealth, more equity, more justice.

For Grandfather Cosimo, like so many other poor peasant soldiers, to become "wealthy" meant to become the owner of land. The only trouble was that landownership in our southern region of Italy was not easily accomplished.

Over centuries, what began as small tracts of individual pieces of land, worked by local farmers, merged into unified territories under the ownership and rule of larger landowners. The large landowner's goal was to subvert the territories of others and develop defenses and tools to control and profit from his own territories. Since the Middle Ages, the building and growth of the region's farmhouses, both those of the peasants and the large landowners, reflected this economic infrastructure, which remained unchanged for centuries, ending finally in the latter half of the twentieth century.

What were these farms like?

Central to the farmhouse was the courtyard around which were built the various necessary buildings: the house itself, the stables and barns, and the storehouses. The houses ranged from modest country homes to *masserie* (fortified farmhouses), typically with a watchtower, which also served as the region's defense structures. It was during the latter half of the eighteenth century that many landowners saw the advantage of exploiting the land for major profit, not just for agricultural purposes. As the defensive purpose of the masserie waned, they were transformed into villas or holiday homes that gradually developed into small holiday villages where city dwellers could escape the heat of summer. The most daring owners added doors, balconies, gazebos, and gardens around the farmhouses. Some houses were even decorated with stucco and frescoes, an unheard-of embellishment in the spartan rural areas. Many of these former masserie were transformed into little architectural jewels.

Who were the owners?

They were gentlemen who could live on rich revenues in a time when most people dined on dried figs. The peasants, biased by the unconscious conditioning of lifelong servitude, respected and envied the landowners, who were often rough and educated only to a certain extent. Nevertheless, to the peasant they appeared refined and god-like. If a landowner's dwelling was in a nearby town, he would visit his masseria weekly, riding a horse-pulled carriage. The visit lasted long enough to include some quick supervision, perhaps to pick the best of the farm produce, to listen to claims and disputes, and do some hunting. Commonly, the gentlemen landowners had the reputation for being kind, benevolent, and tolerant. They could afford to be that way; the dirty work was left to their subjects.

Some of the spirit of the fortified masserie, however, has clung to all of our souls. For a Salentinian, the house and ideally the attached plot of land were one's reign, a safe haven from the chaos of the outside world. It was the place that stood for all one's worth, a symbol of independence linked to a mythical alimentary self-sufficiency.

Luciana says: *Today, many masserie have been restored and made into tourist lodgings.* **L'Astore Masseria**, *located in the town of Cutrofiano, is not just a five-star hotel but also a working farmhouse, where you can also visit the ancient and well-preserved olive oil mill, frantoio ipogeo, below the masseria grounds, built in the 1700s. Through holes in the ground, the farmworkers would drop the freshly picked olives, which were stored in a separate room for each type. You can also eat lunch within the restored walls of the old farmhouse. Next to the frantoio ipogeo, the Benegiamo family, the current owners, maintain an underground wine cellar to store the barreled wines.*
Info: http://www.lastoremasseria.it/index.php?lang=en

My grandfather Cosimo was a lucky one. He returned from the war with two medals and that was it. Salento hadn't changed at all. Yet the time was right for him and his family to take a plot of land under a contract with the landowner. The contract was the *colonia*, and it was the landowner's last trick. The peasants didn't have to depend on anyone. They didn't have to pay rent for the land they worked—ah, but the contract said that they owed the landlord a share of the products, a share ranging from two-thirds to four-fifths of the crops they grew. Those who worked the land in this way, like my grandfather Cosimo, were known as *furese*, the word for peasant in the local dialect. It is easy to understand that the furese had little to gain and the landowner little to lose. If the season was favorable, the crops would thrive, helping the peasant earn the "king's share" painlessly. But if there was no rain, if hail destroyed the young plants, if one of the innumerable threats that curse agricultural work hit, then the furese and their families were left in dire need and often in debt.

In doing research for this book, I browsed through the few fading black-and-white photographs that keep witness to the uneventful lives of my father's family.

Here is one of my grandfather with my grandmother Maria and my aunt and uncle. My father and other aunt were not yet born.

My grandfather was not short in stature for that time. He was one of the tallest in his extended family. Nevertheless, if he were alive today, I would have to look down on him, and my brother is at least a foot-and-a-half taller than he was. In the photograph, my grandfather assumes a highly dignified pose, and the fake background of the photographer's studio only adds to an apparent uneasiness. He had probably been at the barbershop in preparation for the special occasion of having his family's picture taken, and he is wearing his good clothes, those meant for church occasions, such as weddings and funerals. On close examination, I see that he looks *tarchiato*, stocky and dark-skinned. The portrait could bear the caption "Portrait of the Furese as a Young Man." My grandfather must have been in his early twenties because my aunt and uncle in the photograph are young children, yet to me, he already looks old: a furese, tall in his time, but short by today's standards. In a few years his back would arch. Hard labor and fatigue would twist his bones.

Digging deeper into Grandfather Cosimo's story, we learn more about the man and his dedication to his family.

At that time, mothers dreamed for their daughters to marry an *artieri*, an artisan or craftsman, but certainly not a furese. A furese's main concern was to find a daily job, a *sciurnata*. Every evening, the main square of the village became a market where human bodies were on display. My grandfather Cosimo would be there with the other men, wearing a *coppola*, the traditional local cap, waiting to be picked by a *patruno* (middleman) or by any landowning farmer who might need help. For the landowners, choosing and keeping a strong, resilient, and hassle-free worker was vital. The *patruni* personally knew each one of the furese.

At dawn, my grandfather and the other hired laborers would leave home and head to the employer's plot of land, carrying on their shoulders their own shovels. They walked back only after sunset, exhausted and hungry yet often too tired to eat, too hungry to sleep. They quickly refreshed themselves with a bucket of water just out of the well and then returned again to the square in the evening to sell their work for the next day. The shovel they carried had an olive-wood handle, worked, shaped, and polished by constant handling. The blade was rounded. The tool was heavy at four to five kilos (around ten pounds), and in the most difficult of the peasant work—the so-called *scatina*, an unchaining or loosening of the soil—it was lifted over the head, then dropped to cut open the hard-as-clay clods, then raised again, freeing its mouthful of stubborn dirt, over and over under the relentless heat of the sun.

During the summer months, when less work was required, hundreds of furese like my grandfather were hired for *lu messi*, the hay harvest. This work brought them on foot to the plains of the province of Foggia, north of Salento, or to the region of Basilicata, to the west of Puglia. There they would find accommodation and basic food to support them as they worked the landowner's field or at his masseria. It was hard work for weeks and months, sleeping in the stables or under the trees and the stars. At summer's end, the furese would return, carrying back their tools and a salary barely sufficient to pay the arrears to the landowner and the grocer's bill. Some saved part of the food they were served by the owner of the masseria, local cheese and wine, to bring to their families as a special treat from "abroad," together with mussels they might have gathered as they passed by Porto Cesareo on the Salento coast.

On Sundays, other than church and perhaps some card-playing with friends and relatives, most furese pursued their dream of becoming landowning farmers by doing extra work on their own family fields, called *macchie* (spots or stains) because they were dotted with large and small slabs of the white, calcareous limestone common to Salento. Their presence made the land less suitable for cultivation, forcing the furese to use every square meter, even down to the cavities of rocks in the field. They attacked the land with mattocks, shovels, and sledgehammers, cracking and breaking the limestone until it finally fell into smaller pieces, which were then plowed, hoed, and scoured in seemingly pointless, never-ending labor as the land continued to vomit more and more stones.

There is a saying: *La roccia di macchia è più dura dell'acciaio, ma meno dura della nostra pelle. La macchia si prende l'anima.* The stony ground of the macchia is harder than steel, yet not as hard as our skin. The macchia takes your soul.

But in Salento, we also say that each stone helps raise a wall or build a home. Stones were extracted, carried, and neatly laid on top of one another to form farm shelters of dry masonry called *trulli* (houses of stone); *pajare*, *frunieddhari*, or *muri a secco*, stone walls without mortar that surround the macchie; or simply *specchie* (heaps of stones). In this way, the furese built the landscape we see today throughout much of Salento, with trees planted in wall niches and on terraces hewn from the hillsides, with crops in the midst of small clearings surrounded by stones that remain stubbornly in place.

Grandfather Cosimo's macchia was located between our town of Taviano and the town of Mancaversa on the Ionian Sea. It was not enough land to provide a living for our family, so he had to work first for someone else, and only after a hard day's work with the hoe was he able to walk or bicycle to his own macchia. His land was very harsh to cultivate, with sparse almond trees, huge slabs of white stone, plenty of cac

ti, and harmless but numerous snakes. The only water had to be carried from the town's fountains. Nevertheless, my grandfather eventually became a full owner of his macchia, a feat that he, like many other furese, regarded as a longed-for conquest. Sadly, with the passage of time and in spite of all efforts, his spot of land never ceased disgorging stones and has remained little more than the original "stain" on the ground that marked its beginning. The land has been all but abandoned by my grandfather's side of the family, having served in the end only as fertile ground for interfamily squabbles about its ownership.

countryside near Diso

I remember my grandfather Cosimo as a stern man. When we visited and he was at home, he could not be bothered to play with us. He was probably too old and tired. My father addressed him as *signuria*, a show of respect. My grandmother and my aunt anticipated his every wish and need. They were proud of the little comfort they had attained. To me, they seemed blind to the outside world. They stuck to and treasured what were luxuries from the past—a reclining chair, ancient and old-fashioned furniture, kitchenware, and pottery—not because they couldn't afford to make changes but because they were living in the past, free from the struggles of those times; their possessions served as silent, if misleading, witnesses to the post-war promise of more wealth, more equity, and more justice for all Italians.

HOT BREAD AND GREENS

Pane caldo con i verdi

Luciana and Carlo each write about the hard lives of the Salentini who worked in the fields. Though times have changed, the simple eating habits have remained the same. Even today, one will see older women searching for wild chicory in the fields outside of small towns in Salento. Hot Bread and Greens is as satisfying now as it was years ago, eaten alone or accompanying another dish. Serves 2.

Ingredients:
1 lb chicory (or any other tangy leafy green)
Stale bread, cut into 1- to 2-inch cubes
2–4 garlic cloves, coarsely minced
¼ cup olive oil
Salt to taste
Crushed red pepper
1 cup cannellini beans, cooked or canned (optional)

Wash the greens well and then boil or steam them in a saucepan until limp, about 3 to 5 minutes.

Drain the greens and sauté them in a frying pan with the remaining ingredients—olive oil, garlic, salt, crushed red pepper, and pieces of bread—until the bread is toasted to a golden brown.

Serve warm.

For a more substantial dish, once the bread is a golden brown, add cooked cannellini beans to the sautéing ingredients and continue cooking until all is warm.

STAINS ON THE LAND

Not only is the land in Salento fertile with minerals, it is also rich in history and family lore. The land of my maternal grandfather, Vincenzo, unlike the land acquired by Grandfather Cosimo, has been in the family for over two centuries. I often went to it as a child to help with the sowing, weeding, and harvesting of produce. Grandfather Vincenzo's land was more fertile than Cosimo's, although it, too, had begun as a macchia, a small plot of land dotted with large and small slabs of limestone given to peasants to work after each day's labor for the big landowners. Vincenzo's land responded to the breakup of stones, and, in turn, it provided our family with endless vegetables and fruits. The spot of land I inherited from Vincenzo also had a grove of olive trees; meek, patient, strong, and resilient, like the early peasants who cared for them.

olive grove and shed

The peasants' workday lasted from six to ten hours, depending on the kind of contract that bound them to the land, the season, and the harvest. Yet they had time to take care of their own small plots of land, to till their *ortale*, the garden where the family grew herbs, lettuces, tomatoes, and a *pergola* of grape vines to provide shade in the summer afternoons. Sometimes there was an orange or lemon tree. But they also had time to spend with family, to tell tales to children and grandchildren, to teach them, to preserve memories; time to maintain strong and durable relationships with close neighbors and distant relatives.

I wonder how the peasants managed to do it all. Their work meant long walks. Before dawn they would walk or cycle from home to the first field, then from that to the other and so on. On the farms, they carried heavy things: canisters with water for irrigation or containers full of harvested fruits or olives. They used short, heavy shovels and hoes that, over time, contorted their backbone in such a way that you could recognize these slaves of the land from their bowed posture, as if paying a life-long penance, unable to see the sun or look a fellow human in the eye.

Luciana's grandfather's tools

Where did they find the time and will? Today, I steal the few hours I dedicate to my land from a number of commitments. I can drive there comfortably. It takes me no more than five minutes. I have a powerful pump installed in the well. Irrigation is no longer a nightmare. I can buy new tools. As a matter of fact, I often do, and most of them end up hanging unused, awkwardly colorful and bright in the dust-covered storage shed, next to the labor- and time-consuming ancient tools. The effect is that of a Polaroid next to an old sepia portrait.

Moreover, we now have technology and cheap chemicals at our disposal to make a farmer's life easier—though I personally have never taken advantage of these options, either out of laziness or distrust, or even stubbornness. I need to prove to myself that I can do it the old way. I don't care if my fruit and my beans could look better. They couldn't taste better!

So, I wonder, were the peasants' days longer? Was their clock ticking at a slower pace? Their time was dilated; ours is compressed.

seed and chaff sifters

So many fields near mine lie unkempt; I sometimes wonder whether their owners might have actually forgotten them. After all, if you don't have bills to remind you, and you want to avoid cleaning the mud from your shoes and clothes, it becomes very easy to forget what the land has meant to your parents and ancestors. Perhaps owners have moved to *Altitalia*, high Italy, the more prosperous, industrial north— also dubbed by some *Altr'italia*, "the other Italy."

If you need something in small villages like Taviano, your best option is to broadcast your voice. I once circulated the news that I could gladly use some help with my fields, under any condition. A couple of people knocked at my door. They asked if the field was close enough to the town, if it had electric power, if it had a well, if water was available year round.

One said he would give it a try. He would use some of the land to grow some legumes or vegetables for himself—no share for me. In return, he would take care of the place, keep it neat, and undertake the work that needed to be done to maintain the trees: pruning, harvesting, clearing weeds, and keeping away the pests. Old farmers, friends of my late grandfather, were outraged when they heard the news. I was giving away my land! What kind of a deal was that? Unheard of! The new tenant would use land, power, water; he would keep all of the produce and I, the owner, would share only the expenses? They shook their heads in disbelief, as if witnessing the breaking of divine rules.

However, my experiment didn't last. My tenant farmer kept the land for less than two years, then gave me back the keys and tools and admitted defeat. He couldn't manage to run everything alongside his other occupations. He lived in my same compressed, ever-ticking time. Land requires and absorbs too much of it.

It is OK if you grow what's necessary for your family. Other than that, it doesn't pay. It only costs. Selling what you grow is not profitable; margins are so narrow. Supermarkets offer on display bottled olive oil, packaged flour, bags of potatoes, and canned beans that—despite the long distribution chain—

the customer can buy for even less than the products extracted or bought direct from the field. Of course, they won't taste the same, they will have no smell, you don't want to know where they came from, and you'd better ignore the biology of how they were produced. But that's how it is. Economics rule.

Anise gone to seed

ape car

There is a little shed on my land. Inside the shed, there are terra-cotta tiles, thick white walls, and tables made out of old wine barrels, and a tribe of resident geckos, serving as mute guardians. Outside, whitewash paint peels off showing the underlying hand-carved bricks. An old medlar tree serves to shade a porch, and the surrounding yard is scattered with what real peasants (like Grandpa) would call "*sciji*," useless things with no other purpose in life than to be decorative. (Still, is beauty ever purposeless?)

Luciana's garden shed

Despite all my efforts at entering the furese (peasant) frame of mind, I cannot but plan and design in order to be able in the summer to breakfast under a vine-draped arbor next to the softly scented jasmine and a yellow lemon tree.

All around, a dry stone wall and prickly pear cacti frame my land. In my mind, I see the land as shared by four distinct actors, each playing a different role. To the south is the modest orchard of seventy olive trees with some almond and other fruit trees mixed in. To the north and near the shed are rows of ancient, gnarled fruit trees. Then there are the rows of garden vegetables that I try to cultivate and maintain. And finally, there is a major open space in the center that was used by my grandfather Vincenzo for seasonal, rotated crops, such as potatoes, wheat, and the like. That larger area has been barren since I got the land. Plowing, fertilizing, sowing, and irrigating that extension is beyond my forces (and my know-how).

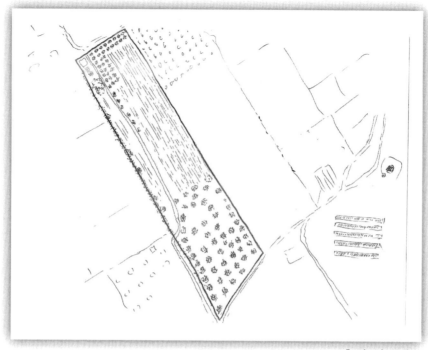

Luciana's garden

My California friends marvel at the variety of fruit trees that the land accommodates. There are figs, pomegranates, persimmons, peaches, apricots, cherries, kiwis, walnuts, almonds, plums, apples, pears, berries, and, of course, olives. They all grow in the stone-cleared grounds, along with a variety of ancient fruits whose names barely survive—fruits that have succumbed to the rules of trade and market under the blows of selective targeted breeding and hybridization; not sufficiently uniform in size and color nor big and shiny enough. The market has traded genuineness and flavor for the appealing, tasteless look. Along with many other concerned farmers here, I intend to reintroduce a few species and cultivars. It is hard and slow work, though rewarding when it comes to finally taste the results.

I make a point in resisting temptations. I have developed a policy of "Salentinization" on my land. I am trying to preserve what has been there for many decades and is now threatened by apparent lack of purpose (the murmurings of my modern friends: Why grow these small, oddly shaped brownish pears when you can have the fashionable variety easily available at the local supermarket? Why keep those giuggiolo trees that spread their thorny offspring all over? And what about the bitter almond trees? Why don't you get rid of all the prickly pear cacti that stand as sentinels along, on, and in the dry stone walls?

And what on earth do you keep a carob tree for?). I try to explain that to me they are like the old, torpid, almost-blind pets that have been in your home for ages. How can I tell them that I call each and every tree, bush, and cactus by name?

But life goes on, and I realize that a plot of land cannot be kept as a museum. I have been thinking of enlarging my shed to allow me to spend spring afternoons in a hammock alongside, perhaps, a small pool. But Taviano's urban plan forbids any new construction on family fields. I worry. A truck would carry construction materials. The truck might hit the trees. I would need to have piping and wires go to and from the enlarged shed. Maybe, after all, I should make changes aimed at maintenance only. Change something so you do not have to change everything. I have seen way too many things change, leaving little or nothing of their old selves behind. Like unwritten memories, those are things that die forever. That is why I resist change. That is why I write. And dream.

Luciana says: *In addition to writing and dreaming, I love to read, both in Italian and in English. My American friends say I am a voracious reader. Two of my favorite bookstores in Salento are* **Libreria Dante Alighieri**, *on Via Matino, in Casarano, and* **Liberrima**, *on Via Vittorio Emanuele II, in Lecce. There is also a charming bookstore in Otranto that my American friends frequent on Via Padre L. Scupoli, in the historic center of town.*

FAVA BEANS WITH BITTER GREENS

Fave e cicoria

The first time we were served this dish was in a small family-run restaurant located just outside the city walls of Lecce. *Fave e cicoria* is a good example of *cucina casalinga* or *casareccia*, meaning "home-style cooking." Our server approached the table with one bowl of steaming-hot pureed fava beans and a separate bowl of piping-hot *cicoria* or chicory, bitter greens. She dribbled a liberal amount of olive oil on top of each one. Then she filled a tablespoon with the fava beans and some of the deep green chicory. She turned to our seatmate, a good friend, and said, "Make a wish," and then spoon-fed him the first bite.

Ingredients:
2 cups fava beans, dried and peeled*
Sea salt as needed
½ cup extra virgin olive oil (or more, if needed)
1 lb bitter greens—chicory, wild dandelion, broccoli rabe, or turnip greens
3–4 garlic cloves, minced (optional)
One thick slice per guest of country-style bread, toasted or lightly fried in olive oil
Water sufficient to cover the beans (6 cups)

Place the fava beans in a large saucepan and add fresh water to cover. Cook them over a low heat. As the beans start to boil, they will foam up. Skim the foam with a wooden spoon. Once the foam stops rising, add a good pinch of salt, cover, and bring to a full boil.

As the beans cook down, stir them frequently with a long-handled wooden spoon. They will gradually dissolve into the cooking liquid. This should take about an hour. Stir frequently, as the fava beans dissolve to keep them from sticking to the bottom of the pan and burning.

Do not overcook, as the mixture will dry out and become hardened. Add more water as necessary until the beans are completely dissolved into a puree of just enough consistency to keep the mixture from becoming runny.

Stir in ¼ cup of the olive oil. Add salt to taste.

While the beans are cooking, clean the greens thoroughly in several changes of water. Place them in a large kettle and boil them in a small bit of water, including that which clings to their leaves, until they are thoroughly cooked and tender, about 20 minutes.

(At this point, if you choose to use the optional garlic, sauté the minced garlic until soft in a separate skillet with three additional tablespoons of olive oil, add the cooked greens, mix well, and continue sautéing for an additional 10 minutes or until the greens have taken up the garlic flavor. In Salento, this process is known as "twice cooking" the greens).

Once the greens are cooked and tender, drain them in a colander and transfer them to a large serving bowl. Dress with the remaining olive oil and toss to mix well.

To serve the *fave e cicoria*, place a toasted or fried slice of bread onto a serving plate or in a shallow bowl, spoon the fava puree on top of the toast, and place a serving of the greens alongside the puree. Dribble a bit of olive oil on both beans and greens. Make a wish and take a bite.

Makes 6 servings as a first course.

*Bob's Red Mill sells a 20-ounce (4 cups) package of naturally blanched and peeled fava beans.

Audrey says: *Just outside the Lecce city walls is the restaurant* **Le Zie, Trattoria Cucina Casareccia**, *located in the downstairs room of a house. Specialties, referred to as* "cucina povera" *(cooking of the poor), are all local dishes, such as the fava beans and bitter greens,* siambotto *(a vegetable stew), and stuffed calamari. The place fills up quickly with local Italians so make reservations. Once you arrive, ring the doorbell to gain admittance. (Viale Colonnello Archimede Costadura 19)* Info: http://www.lezietrattoria.com/

OUR LIQUID GOLD

It has been said that Homer called olive oil "liquid gold." Olives have been cultivated throughout the Mediterranean for thousands of years, even before written language was invented. We know that the earliest oil containers found in Crete and Greece date back to around 3500 BC. Like alchemists, Salentinians continue to produce this "liquid gold" from olives that often come from ancestral trees, many of them over 400 years old.

In fact, Salento is one huge olive grove that blankets the land with its silvery cloak. Within Puglia, I contend (without prejudice, of course) that the southern province of Salento makes the finest oil from the finest olive trees. The scale of our olive cultivation ranges from families like ours, with less than a hundred trees, harvested by hand, which produce enough oil for our family and a few friends, to large-scale commercial farms that produce export quantities. During the time of year when olives are being harvested and pressed in the villages, the smell of their fruit lingers in the air.

Olive groves stand mute during most of the year, neither disturbed nor in need of attention. We are reminded of them when, late in spring and early summer, they begin to flourish.

The flowers, solitary or aggregated, fragrant and small, are similar to strings of prayer beads or pearls. After olive trees have flowered, the fruit starts to develop, again with little if any human help. Olives begin their lives green and hard. As they mature, their color changes to yellow-green, then to deep purple, and finally to black. All along this process the levels of acidity, antioxidants, and carotenoids change. When the fruit is unripe, oil yield is low, and the oil can be quite bitter. As the fruit matures, the yield increases and the oil sweetens.

Although there is little consensus among Salentinians as to the ideal stage to begin harvesting, it is generally agreed that when the olives begin to fall freely off the tree, the peak time for harvest is over, and the resultant oil will be of poorer quality. For centuries the harvest was the women's job. They bent under the groves from dawn to dusk, picking the droopers from low hanging branches, one by one, with their agile fingers, putting them into *vimini* (baskets; each woman had her own), which when full were emptied into a canvas sack that was then carried home by the men or on muleback. Back in time, it was a sociable event: friends and family would come together to help out and gossip as they worked and then shared lunch together. The work is not hard, even for first-timers and amateurs. The fall weather is usually mild and pleasant; no need to carry heavy baskets, to handle equipment, to kneel, to use much physical strength or resistance. Compared to the harvest of other crops, mainly done under the hot summer sun, harvesting olives is a relaxing walk in the park. All in all, it is pain-free and extremely satisfying work. And the best part is that in a few days' time you get to enjoy the delicious, brand-new olive oil.

Luciana says: *In the town of Carmiano there is an olive oil mill called* **Schirinzi,** *where olives are cold-pressed, which is not very common. The oil that is milled this way preserves the taste and aroma of the fruit. In addition, the oil goes through a process of natural sedimentation that leaves it non-filtered and more genuine. You can also take a guided tour of the Schirinzi plant, where you will learn about harvesting, the techniques of the oil extraction, and how olive oil is produced. And you will have the opportunity to taste this "liquid gold." Via Copertino 153 - 73041, Carmiano (LE) Italy* Info: http://www.pugliaextravirginoliveoil.com/

Nowadays, we can shake branches of the olive tree with a shaker bar attached to a tractor or use a pneumatic rake or similar mechanized system to get the olives off the tree. More traditionally, however, the olives are picked by hand or shaken free with a stick and gathered into nets laid out on the ground around the tree trunks. Olives picked by hand may also be put into baskets carried by the workers. Hand-picking and hand-shaking are still the best methods so as not to damage the trees or bruise the fruit. In our family, we believe that the more traditional methods produce the finest extra virgin olive oil as long as the olives are treated with the utmost care and cold pressed quickly.

Unfortunately, growing and harvesting olives for oil these days is not cost-effective, unless you have abundant spare time and efficient, willing help from your family and friends. I am fortunate to have such volunteers in most years. The olive harvest has always been one of my favorite times of the year. In November 2011, my olive groves looked promisingly laden, and I anticipated harvesting an abundant crop that would yield excellent-quality olive oil. I took credit for the increased crop, as I had been managing the trees with extra care by pruning heavily and treating them with copper sulfate spray to protect them from the harsh sirocco winds. I believe the pruning in particular proved beneficial, although for me, it was a very traumatic process.

They say that in order to get the best from our olive trees we need to prune them up high to allow light and air into the center of the tree, which helps prevent pests and diseases from taking hold. Removing dead wood encourages new fruiting wood to emerge and keeps the tree youthful, and finally, pruning helps to keep the tree a manageable size. This proved important in 2011 as we started to harvest with only family members playing the role of professional pickers. I don't mind cutting away growths from the base of the tree—the suckers reduce the vigor of the tree and also make it tricky to put down the catch nets—but I had so far opposed any more invasive pruning work.

However, I was persuaded that more radical pruning was a necessary evil, and two years earlier, during the spring, before my olive trees had started to flower, I surrendered them to the war surgeons.

What my brain said, however, was not what my heart felt. Watching the pruning work in progress was a painful experience. It was nothing like hairdressing or manicure work. As a matter of fact, it shocked me: half a dozen skilled pruners surrounded each tree like opportunistic predators surrounding a victim, armed with blades, saws, scissors, and ropes. They climbed the tree and conquered it. Then, when they had taken hold of it—imagine ten men in the same treetop working furiously—they began an undignified mutilation. Down fell the sawed limbs, still bleeding, like my own wounded heart. Thank God one doesn't need to prune every tree every year! It is only small consolation that at the end the small prunings are gathered for a bonfire and the larger logs sawed into fuel for the home fireplace.

The other key ingredient to a successful harvest is enough workers to do the picking, a task that my family and friends and I have traditionally done by plucking each individual olive by hand before resorting to shaking the branches. We reward ourselves, of course, by frequent breaks for hearty food and drink. In 2011, we scheduled the harvest for the beginning of November to take advantage of a perfect combination of factors: my helpers and I had a few days off because of school holidays; the olives were ripening earlier than usual so the town's olive presses had already begun working; and Saint Martin was expected to bless our work with warm and sunny weather. What is elsewhere known as Indian summer, here we call *l'estate di San Martino* (Saint Martin's summer).

It is exhilarating to look forward to spending so much time outdoors in such a productive endeavor. Our team of pickers that year, at its fullest, consisted of six people. Since they were all "volunteers," I could not act like the lazy landowner who orders everyone around. Rather, as the one experienced, seasoned picker of the group, I directed everyone. At the start of the day, each with a basket, we headed all together toward the olive-laden trees, around seventy of them in regimented rows called *sesti*; *sesto* means "sixth," and six is the average number of meters between olive trees.

We first plucked the lower-hanging olives. Next, we arranged huge bright-green nets under the trees to catch the olives as they were scraped or shaken from the branches with either gloved or bare hands and special long-handled rakes. Finally, after hours of this, we gathered up the nets and tipped the fallen olives into crates.

The children plucked olives from the lower branches or collected them from the nets, emptying them into their baskets or tins. The older ones climbed high up in the trees to the top branches, with rakes in hand. My twelve-year-old nephew Gabriele's insistence on climbing to the top amidst protests that he would fall showed me that the olive harvest was in his blood. As director of pickers, I allowed him to do the work the way he wanted.

The children worked fast and furiously. I didn't think they could work so hard and for so long! For such a small group, we worked quickly and gathered many olives. We stayed until it started to get too dark to see the olives. Then we returned the next day to do it all over again.

Once the olives were picked, we took them to one of the town olive presses. The olives had to be delivered for pressing within twenty-four hours of harvesting. Otherwise, the fruit begins to ferment and the flavor of the oil is tainted. At the height of harvesttime in our village, there are long lines of horse-drawn carts, tractor-pulled wagons, and other open carriers filled with olives, each one waiting its turn to disgorge its fruit into the presses, where the harvest process is completed. Each of us stays with the fruit to make sure our own olives are not mixed with the inferior olives of our neighbors. We watch until the pressing has ended and our own olive oil has been segregated into large glass jars ready for transport home.

Luciana says: *In Taviano, on Via Castelforte,* **Frantoio Calzolaro** *is another traditional neighborhood mill that doubles as both a grape and an olive press, changing its focus depending on the harvest—early September for grapes, mid- to late October for olives. Local farmers form a line outside the entrance to the press, each with his cart laden with grapes or olives direct from the harvest. Payment is in enormous bottles of either very fresh wine or delicious olive oil.*

Later in the season, the few remaining olives, aided by the winds, ripen and fall into the nets. The oil from these olives, though, is of lower quality and needs refining. Historically, at the end of the harvest, when the trees had been combed, shaken, and beaten and few olives were left on the branches, the poor wandered from one olive grove to another, picking through the leftover olives hidden among the fallen leaves on the ground.

For my family, the best part of picking olives is our payment in liters of the most delicious oil for family and friends to enjoy until the next year's harvest. The first tasting on a slice of warm bread is a celebration of the fruit's bounty: the yield of a year of nature's work but only a week of our own! Truly, in Salento, we who can bring home enough oil to fulfill our family needs until the following harvest feel as rich as kings. The liquid gold of our olives, not money, has been and will continue to be the measure of our family's well-being.

Luciana's niece, Elisa, at olive harvest

Luciana says: *During the olive harvest months in mid- to late September, you may want to visit a* frantoio *(local olive mill or press). Loads of fresh olives, straight from being plucked off their branches, arrive at our local mill in Taviano. Those that have been picked at the perfect time are uniformly green-ripe. We harvesters cherish them as we would a newborn. We each compare our olives with those in nearby boxes and are flattered, rightfully so, if ours look fresher or plumper. It is the result of the year's weather, of course, but also represents the extra care we take at harvest time: olives picked by hand, especially early, are less likely to separate easily from their branches, making the harvest a time-consuming, tedious operation. But the reward is a better-quality product, since the emerging oil is likely to have a higher antioxidant level with a pronounced* pizzica—*the slight burn at the back of the throat that alerts you to the presence of healthy polyphenols.*

We producers are careful not to let our olives get mixed with those of our neighbors, which may be too ripe or damaged. We watch the process carefully, standing along the line, as extra bits of leaf or twig are removed. The fresh olives are ground into a paste and then go into a mixer where the fresh paste is gently kneaded to encourage the juice to bloom and separate from the olive pulp. The mill is filled with an incredible aroma, much like when you drizzle extra virgin olive oil over a slice of warm, toasted bread. Out of the mixer comes fresh olive juice that is separated yet again: this time it's the oil separating from the fruit liquid. It's a very fresh, high-quality extra virgin olive oil that emerges from the tap. The moment the new oil drips off the line into a waiting container, its iridescent, golden-green, silky viscosity—so hypnotizing and soothing—makes the whole process worthwhile.

The oil is immediately stored in tall stainless steel casks or in green glass demijohns, which will protect it from damaging heat, light, and air. Finally, we proud "parents" can bring it home and secure it in cool cellars. Our local mill is **Frantoio Agronatura di Cazzato Donato & C.,** located on the Via Provinciale, between the towns of Taviano and Melissano.

NETTA'S BEET SALAD

Insalata di barbabietole da Netta

Netta Cacciatore, Luciana's mother, grew up in Taviano. Her father loved to cook, though he would only cook with the vegetables from his garden, the garden that now belongs to Luciana. Netta remembers eating beet salad prepared by her father. In the old days, when her father and others were out in the fields harvesting tomatoes, the beet salad he had brought along would be placed in a straw basket and lowered into a nearby well to keep cool until lunchtime.

Netta surprised us one visit with a freshly made bowl of beet salad. The beets were pink, the potatoes were golden, the slices of light green celery stalks and leaves lay half hidden beneath the beets and potatoes. This recipe serves 5 to 6 people and, if served chilled, is a terrific complement to a hot summer day.

Ingredients:
8–10 beets, red, golden, or pink
4–5 medium-sized yellow potatoes
3 celery stalks, with leaves
3 tbsp white wine vinegar
5 tbsp olive oil
Salt and pepper to taste
10–12 capers (optional)

Boil the beets and potatoes with their skins on. You can boil them together but then your potatoes will turn the color of the beets. When the beets and potatoes are cooked but still firm, peel and cut into 1- to 1½-inch quarters and place in a large bowl.

Chop the celery stalks and leaves into ¼-inch pieces and add to the beets and potatoes. Add capers, if desired.

Make a dressing by mixing together the vinegar, olive oil, and salt.

Add the dressing to the beets, potatoes, and celery, toss lightly, and refrigerate. Serve when cold.

GRANDFATHER VINCENZO AND HIS WIFE

I was raised in the comfortable and reassuring milieu of an extended family. My parents, Netta and Tullio, built their home on top of my maternal grandparents' house. The only boundary between the two houses was two flights of stairs, scaled often on a daily basis. Since my mother was at school teaching every morning, my grandmother cooked for us all, except that my grandpa liked to work the dough to make bread. It was a religious act. He took the loaves to the town oven before dawn. When he returned with the fragrant, fresh-baked bread, he would pick a *ncummatura*, the crispy crust of a side, and hand it to me. I remember the fragrant smell of that bread, the closest thing to heaven in my mind. My grandparents spoiled my sister and brother and me in a big way. The more my parents tried to be tough, taking very seriously their task to raise us to be well-mannered children, the more we would rush downstairs and seek comfort and treats from our grandparents. Downstairs was my grandparents' kingdom.

But who were they?

I remember my grandmother sitting next to a window or going to church with the mandatory kerchief fastened under her chin. She was friendly, yet humble. She was the fourth of seven children, five daughters and two sons, born in the village of Alliste, a few kilometers south of Taviano. Although it is usually easy in a small village to trace the family tree far back to past generations, her surname is unique and no relatives can be found. My guess is that an illegitimate child, my grandmother's father, was given a made-up surname. He was the first in that branch of the family. Now, too late for human memory or paper records, unwritten memories have deleted whole lives.

At a time when a household's wealth was measured by the man's capacity to work the land and by the woman's honesty, modesty, chastity, and needlework skills, money played little, if any, role. One of my grandmother's brothers died at a very early age, and the one remaining brother, against his parents' will, wanted to try his luck in *L'America*. His situation must have been desperate. His sisters supported him, even though he took some of the family money set aside for their dowries when he left by ship for Montevideo. Over time, his letters became fewer and fewer as hope and enthusiasm dwindled. His sisters secretly sent him money. Eventually, he disappeared and was never heard from again.

One by one, my grandmother and three of her sisters married. All but one: my blind aunt, Nunziata. They all, except my grandma, outlived their husbands. They all had big families, giving birth to plenty of children, who, in turn, produced small armies of grandchildren.

My maternal grandmother married less successfully than her sisters, or it seemed that way at first.

Her husband, my grandfather and godfather Vincenzo, was far from being the son-in-law parents would fancy for their daughters. He was tall, handsome, good-humored, and strong, all of which he knew all too well and was eager to make the most of it. He glowed with vitality, always willing to travel, meet new people, read, learn, and enjoy all aspects of life, including young women. He ran away with a few of them, and even today family members and friends draw a curtain of embarrassed silence when it comes to his *fuitine*, escapes with potential marriage partners whom he never intended to marry.

I have asked, more or less discreetly, how Grandfather Vincenzo came to settle down with my grandmother. She, quiet and soft-spoken, was not the kind to draw attention. I remember her as old-fashioned with an extreme concern for decency. She used to keep a close eye on me from her front window, watching my comings and goings when I was a teenager. She always asked me where I was going and disapproved of my going out at all. I bitterly resented her intrusions into my already limited privacy and social life. When I was little, she used to tell me, "I only want to live until I see you married . . . *ulia campu tte visciu zita*" in dialect. I have disappointed her big time.

Someone told me that Grandfather Vincenzo was forced to settle down with my grandmother. I do not know if that's true. All I know is that in his later years, he cherished her, never let her down, and when she passed away, his life ended. After the funeral, he locked the door to his home and kept it locked for good, materially and spiritually. Joy disappeared from his life and the smile from his lips. His only outings were to his fields. He cooked for himself, watched TV, and was aware of what was going on in the world, but he was quiet and distant.

One of my grandpa's friends greeted each morning by looking up to the heavens with the angry yet triumphant gesture of bent arm and clenched fist, addressing God, death, age, and fate: "*E puru osci t'aggiu futtutu*"—"I've beaten you another day!" My grandfather, on the other hand, shook his head in disapproval at such outbursts. He found them silly. After the death of his wife, life's fists pummeled him every day. He refused to fight back.

AUNT ANITA: EMBROIDERING A LIFE

Since her parents' deaths, Aunt Anita has lived alone. She never married, though by no means for lack of suitors. She was a beautiful girl, given the beauty standards and canons of that time in Salento during the early 1900s. The requirements and the expectations for a young woman to be a desirable wife and, above all, an acceptable daughter-in-law were many. They included, not necessarily in this order, a spotless reputation, which meant no scandals about her or her immediate family members, a modest attitude, and decent clothing. Church attendance was a plus.

Clothing was important not so much to highlight the girl's attractiveness but rather because it was the best evidence of her needlework abilities. This talent was the only training considered suitable for a decent girl. The division of labor in peasant families assigned to the women the weaving and sewing of clothes and household linens. The younger girls decorated the items with various types of embroidery. The marriage trousseau, a certain number of pieces with specific names, uses, colors, and destinations, was the main concern and the most important task for girls. In preparations for any wedding party, the trousseau was put on display as part of the dowry of the future bride. This dowry was the only asset that could rightfully be handed down the female line.

Girls were sent to a *mescia*, a qualified teacher of tailoring who typically hosted classes in her own house in rooms set aside for that purpose. Knitwear, fine embroidery with bobbing and needle lace, top-quality embroidered fabric, and needle-stitch lace were all produced in these workrooms.

Groups of girls—crowds in the case of *mescie* with high reputations—attended these informal classes, where they not only learned to cut and sew, mend, attach buttons, and adapt patterns but were also introduced to loom work and the art of embroidery. Of course, these students also enjoyed moments of all-female chitchat. Bent over their cloth pieces, they exchanged information about the incidents of everyday life: childcare, popular medicinal remedies, how to prepare that special dish, along with giggling comments on this young man or that one. They were separated only by half-drawn curtains from representatives of the other gender who promenaded up and down before the workshop windows, strutting and showing off for the girls.

The reputation of a girl as being good at needlework and housework circulated in the village and even reached neighboring towns. It was her true dowry. Women checked on each other's work, mothers praised their daughters' skills, girls envied and tried to emulate their friends' patterns and styles. Each tried to both keep and steal secrets. The girls' training was a passport to the world outside, to new lives as married women, which, in turn, was viewed as a guarantee that shared dreams could come true. The *mescia*'s house was the anteroom for new life.

In the last few decades the tradition of the trousseau has been fading away. Unlike my aunt Anita, who is my father's older sister, my mother is unable to use a needle. As an only child, she was brought up expecting to be served. I once heard someone say that for the standards of her time, she was spoiled and pampered. Most of my friends and classmates were taught basic mending and knitting and happily learned some needlework. I learned from my mother, which means that I cannot hold a needle properly either. My grandmother felt responsible for the neglect and missed no chance to fill my sister's hope chest and mine. My grandmother carefully selected all the required items, including the fabric, design, and embroidery patterns.

Except for weddings, the only reason my grandmother would travel by car was to visit the few shops that sold acceptable-quality linens that met her standards. Even then she had to instruct the embroiderer on how this or that item had to be made and which was to be for my sister, Marinella, and which was to be for me. Our initials were then embroidered on each piece. All birthdays, celebrations, and good marks at school were rewarded with boxes of gifts that have hardly seen the light of day. Both my sister and I have yet to marry, and as a result, we now have several hope chests, two of which bear the label "First night things!"

My aunt Anita, now eighty-five, recently suffered a fractured hip and has just come home after the first (and hopefully last) hospital visit in her life. She is an independent, strong woman, very proud of her self-sufficiency. She will not accept any assistance: she spent a short period in a private clinic following a physical rehabilitation program, and she could not stand the comfort of the place. Unused to assistance, she could not be persuaded that a health regimen was suitable for someone with an injury. She was homesick, too.

Shortly after her return home, while she was getting used to walking with a cane, I offered to help take the garbage out. It struck me how small and light her garbage bags were. I am ashamed to confess that my family produces in a single day the amount she probably discards in a couple of weeks. Separate collection of household waste will never be an issue for her, since she uses very few plastic items, none disposable. It's not a matter of money; she just does not belong to a consumer society. She cannot be persuaded that disposable items are sometimes cheaper than mending reusable ones; that it is quite a job to even find a shoe repairer, let alone one who can mend hand-woven slippers; that a pair of new slippers would cost less and would be warmer and more comfortable. She does not listen to such arguments.

My aunt Anita was a very good embroiderer. Without seeming to brag about it, she often makes us look at a certain set of linens for which she had used a special *punto*, a stitch with a fancy name. She lets us know where the cloth came from and the thread and how smart she was at copying elaborate designs and patterns, ranging from rococo to baroque to Renaissance styles. Many people in our town know and still remember her fine work. She could turn useless cuttings of cloth fabric into botanical garden baskets of exotic leaves and flowers, chubby *putti* (cherubs), and colorful butterflies.

She was so good that a tradesman who noticed her work recommended her to a producer who proposed that she work to order. She agreed. The purchaser would then send her the cloth, pattern, yarn, and thread. She did the work as requested and the tradesman would then collect the finished items. When she recounts this experience, she never fails to mention, her face aglow, how she managed to pay for her four-door wardrobe, where she still keeps her trousseau, now infused with a terrible blended scent of lavender, camphor, and mothballs. A local carpenter made and assembled the wardrobe in the same room where it stands today. It will always be there. The house's doors are too small to let it out.

When Aunt Anita was in the hospital, I had to go through her belongings inside the wardrobe. Until that time it had been a nightmarish threat every time I walked next to it during my visits. I would try to find a subject of conversation that would possibly distract my aunt's attention from its contents. My sister, my sister-in-law, and I knew well what to expect if she got started on it. Inside there were small cuttings of cloth in different fabrics and colors in such bizarre and capricious shapes, so much beauty for beauty's sake.

When given the opportunity, my aunt would explain that the purchaser's firm did not collect the unused leftovers, and of course, it would be a pity and a shame to let them be wasted, so she used the yarn by tying all the short pieces together with invisible knots. She covered every reusable piece of fabric with imitations of the patterns they sent her or with original designs. Some of her work deserves a place in a museum or in a gallery: dragons and multicolor butterflies, ripe pomegranates, baskets with all sorts of flowers, among which multitudes of birds flapped their wings, so true-to-life that you could almost hear them singing.

This absorbing extra work had to be performed by candlelight so as not to steal time and eyesight from the work she was being paid to make. From her early teens to middle age, she served her father and brothers, took care of her mother, and did all the housework. Embroidery was her only entertainment. Her entire life was spent in preparing for a new life that never came into being.

Still, if you ask her, Aunt Anita talks about her past expectations with no resentment. On the contrary, she speaks with a relief derived from what we call the "afterwards wisdom." She discreetly hints at this or that suitor who had pursued her (I have lost count of them), this other who had even been "talking" with her—meaning that his courtship had received an initial approval by her father/brothers and had been, for a while, tolerated by her. Inevitably, the reminiscence ends with "They told me he is dead now" or "has become blind" or "has lost his mind" or "beats his wife" or "has disappeared in a coal-mining incident."

I guess she feels she was spared. I think she sees her life as a superior design, like one of her embroidered pieces. And she is happy to conform to it. "*Fazza Diu*" (let God see for us), she repeats. He surely knows better.

Aunt Anita's embroidery

In the past, the ancient techniques of embroidery were taught as part of an inheritance, passed on from generation to generation. Like memories, they are now fading away, and the task of safeguarding past traditions has now fallen onto the few who recognize the value of those skills even during a time when the rest of the world seems to view it as work made useless by the modern means of production or, in the best cases, as folklore.

The result is that even the names of fancy *punti* or "lace-stitch" are being lost for good. I tell myself I need to take pictures of my aunt's handicrafts and to tape record her while she describes how they were made. I have not yet done so, in part out of laziness. However, I suspect that behind my tendency to procrastinate lies the belief that such traditions will not be lost, that there is still time for conversation, and that people will continue talking about their lives. Attempting to freeze words or pictures of such traditions on digital memory sounds too much like anticipating their loss.

Luciana says: *A great place to see the traditional weaving process in operation and to purchase handmade Salentinian embroidery and fabrics is the* **Fondazione Le Costantine**, *an all-women enterprise started after World War II to give support and dignity to women. The women still use traditional wood looms and weaving techniques. The foundation is located in the suburb of Casamassella, in the town of Uggiano La Chiesa, just south of Otranto.*

Info: http://www.lecostantine.eu/tessitura/

CHAPTER THREE

David

THE SKETCHER

John Berger, the philosopher and drawer, once wrote, "What do drawings mean to me?" In reply, he answered, "The activity absorbs me. I forget everything else in a way that I don't think happens with any other activity . . ." This is true for me as well. Drawing is a meditation that makes room for only the drawing and me. The end result is not only a personal record of travels but also a memory enhanced by a heightened sense of observation and enjoyment of the experience. Drawing provides a purpose. It satisfies a desire to be creative. And it all fits with my grandfather's advice.

When I was a child sitting on Grandpa's lap, the one thing he would tell me, so often I could predict when he was going to say it, was "You can be anything you want to be and do anything you want to do as long as you put your mind to it." Of course, Grandpa was a self-assured man, very conservative, very independent, and as it became evident to a maturing grandchild, very intolerant of others who might not have been so successful in life. He had left home at the age of fourteen, as there were too many mouths to feed in his family, and he saw no future for himself in his hometown of New Market, Virginia.

Grandpa had dozens of jobs as he grew up. He had been a railroad worker, a newspaper reporter and eventually the publisher of a small-town newspaper, a representative in the Iowa General Assembly, and finally, in California, the owner of a bank that went belly-up during the Great Depression. One year, long after my grandfather and grandmother had settled in Southern California, my mother arrived by train from Colorado with my brother and me. My brother was four years old; I was one. Our father had sent us to live with my mother's parents in California while he reported for military service in Colorado. Soon after we arrived, our father wrote to our mother telling her that he had fallen in love with another woman. Our mother, with help from my grandparents, raised my brother and me.

I say Grandpa was intolerant. Whenever he spoke of African Americans or Mexicans or even Italians, he would use a disparaging name. He admonished us to choose our friends carefully. After my brother graduated from college, he married a girl of Mexican descent. Grandpa refused to attend the wedding and never forgave him. So, while I was raised to believe I could be anything or do anything I wanted if I just put my mind to it, I came perilously close to believing the corollary: that if anyone failed at accomplishing something, they had clearly not put their mind to it—it was their own fault.

Had it not been for my mother and her career as a high school counselor, I might well have turned out just as intolerant as Grandpa. Like him, my mother loved to tell us stories, but hers were often about the kids she met in the high schools where she worked who indeed had failed in so many ways. We learned about the boy who claimed he had missed school because his finger had gotten stuck in a bottle. And about the girl too young and too poor to have a baby, for whom my mother had risked her own job by helping her find a doctor willing to end the pregnancy and allow her to return to a normal life. And, of course, there were stories about the kids who routinely missed school, usually with one or both parents absent, in jail, or working two and three jobs, and inevitably poor. And while my Grandpa may have shown me what was possible in the world, it was my mother's compassion for others less fortunate that helped shape the person I am.

If we have the freedom to choose our labor, it is our chosen field that tends to define who we are. Over the years, I have gained the most satisfaction from work that tends to add value to society. I have been a United States Peace Corps volunteer in Peru, an attorney for the poor in the California-Mexico border town of Calexico, an advisor to the University of Costa Rica on the subject of legal aid for the poor, and an attorney in private practice, whose clients were mostly workers unfairly fired from their jobs. Now, I am a fan of philosophy and cosmology, an amateur sketcher, and occasionally a mediator of employment-related disputes. I am a grandfather to three grandchildren who are acquiring, I hope, a sense of duty to their society.

Over the past ten years or so, as Audrey and I have emerged from our professional careers and returned over and over again to Salento, and as our friendship with the other authors of this book has blossomed, I have become a passionate Salentophile. The rather loose, untutored style of sketching found in this book is a consequence of that background and those passions. It is also influenced both by the newfound freedom afforded by letting go of a law practice and by the lingering effects, not always welcomed, of an adherence to precision from long-ago training in the engineering field.

You may note from looking at the sketches in this book that I am not a trained artist; that while the drawings may convey a sense of their intended subject, they do so rather loosely and with an amateur's hand. I could say that this has been my intention, but it would not be entirely true, for I aspire to draw at least accurately enough to enable the reader to recognize the thing drawn. Beyond that, however, I concede that my goal for most sketches has, from the start, been merely to create a sort of personal journal that records the scenes and places and objects we have seen and pondered during my travels in Salento. The sketches are indeed personal and idiosyncratic; a bonus would be that they are of interest to our own children and grandchildren. Hopefully, they are also an enjoyable complement in this book to our and our friends' writings.

Many drawings were made on blank postcards and sent to family and friends back home. They and others taken from my travel journals are sprinkled throughout the book. What follows are a number of complete pages from the journals that give a flavor, purple prose and all, of our Salentinian experience over the years.

David says: *For the artist, there is a very special place just to the south of Otranto known as the* **Vecchia Cava di Bauxite** *or Old Bauxite Cave. It is a small, year-round seep, or lake, surrounded by rich, reddish-brown earth that is mined by artists from all over Italy and beyond for its use as a pigment base. Bring along a half dozen small jars and collect the fine-grained earth in colors ranging from "sand" to "raw umber" to "sepia" to "mahogany" and a continuum of hues in between. The short dirt road to the Bauxite Cave begins with a left turn, heading south on the Otranto to Santa Maria di Leuca highway, no more than a quarter mile from Otranto. There is no sign, just turn off onto the first dirt road on your left, a hundred meters past the roundabout, and follow your nose to an obvious parking area. Then walk back toward the highway on any one of the many short trails to reach the lake hidden among the trees. It's an enchanting sight, even for the non-artist.*

David says: *The **BAU Institute** offers artists and writers residencies in Salento. These working retreats are for scholars and professionals in the arts. They are hosted in a sixteenth-century stone masseria in the Salento countryside, close to Lecce and the Adriatic Sea. Meals and local excursions are included.* Info: www.bauinstitute.org

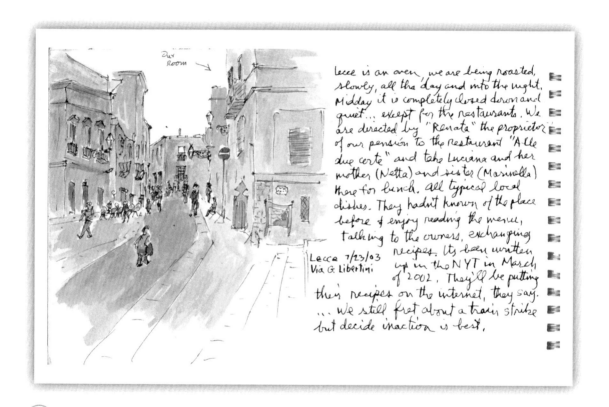

David says: *Between the towns of Torre Specchia and San Foca, on the Adriatic Coast, there are two well-known venues for evening events: **Lido Buenaventura** is known for special Saturday night parties called "Il Sabatone" (The big Saturday) with 'surf rock' music. And **Lido Mamanera** specializes in reggae nights.*

Dates and times for these and all other Salento events during the summer season can be found in either of two widely available publications. Perhaps the best known for checking out what's going on in Salento is the magazine named QuiSalento, found at most newsstands. Also, for information on Salento nightlife, there is the free 2night magazine, typically found in local coffee bars and tourist shops. Both magazines also have online presences.

For the 4th year in a row, we arrive at Otranto and Salento, this time to embark on a book project with our friends. Can we find success? Five authors! Too many cooks spoil the broth? But we have only one cook ... Lucia. And Audrey ... chief author and bottle washer. It will be fun trying.

9·9·06
Otranto

EL NAUTILUS

We've found a B & B here in Sta Caterina — on the opposite side of Salento from Otranto — north of our friends in Mancaversa. Sta Caterina 7·9·10 Fielding
We stroll the 5K seaside promenade between Sta Caterina and Sta Maria al Bagno. Fishing boats share swim beaches. Seafood pasta and pizza. We meet, converse & exchange email addresses with a retired couple from Pescara.

The coast south of Otranto is rocky and windswept, studded with wild flowers. Odysseus and his crew landed here just yesterday.

Sept. 2006

Antico Bar Centrale

Our first apartment in Otranto, above the bar. We stayed here while looking for a larger place that might accomodate visiting friends.

Antico Bar Centrale, Otranto 9.22.05

David says: *If you're wondering where to go for nightlife in Salento, here are a couple of suggestions, keeping in mind that most anywhere in Salento is within an hour's or less drive from anywhere else in Salento.*

Solatio is a lounge bar with a view terrace directly over the rocks on the edge of the Ionian Sea. It is located on the coast about thirty minutes south of Gallipoli, in the town of Torre Suda. During the evening, local and national disc jockeys perform, playing popular Italian and international sounds for the primarily youthful crowd. We met Carlo's son Davide there one evening, just by chance. Another time, we joined Luciana and her niece Elisa at Solatio for drinks and an appetizer at sunset. Cocktails are well made, if a tad expensive, but the view of the sea at sunset is unbeatable. The scene is lively after dark.

Sunset Café is another spot in the same vein as Solatio. The Sunset Café is located in the nearby town of Capilungo, just south of Torre Suda. It is a bar and lounge constructed entirely of wood and also situated on the coastal rocks with a spectacular view. According to Davide, the scene at the Sunset Café is more relaxed than that of Solatio. The disc jockeys focus on contemporary rock, and there is occasional live music—all at popular prices. Like Solatio, the Sunset Café is open and lively almost every night of the summer season from July to September.

David says: *For nightlife in the town of Gallipoli, visit* **Parco Gondar***, a former amusement park turned into a large arena for concert events where world-renowned artists perform during the summer season. The venue also has a smaller room with walls of knotty pine that features underground electro music. Food and beer are served. Admission is free for smaller events; larger events typically charge admission fees. Lecce also has a number of nightlife venues. Our friend Davide suggests* **Caffè Letterario***, a small but well-known hipster café with high-quality wines and liqueurs. It has occasional art/photo exhibitions as well as acoustic sets. Another very famous spot in Lecce is* **Urban Cafè***, in Piazzetta Santa Chiara, an area known as the heart of Lecce nightlife. You can also stroll the Via Federico D'aragona (called 'street of the pubs' by locals). There you will find* **Road 66***, an American-style pub with several types of beer and small food plates.*

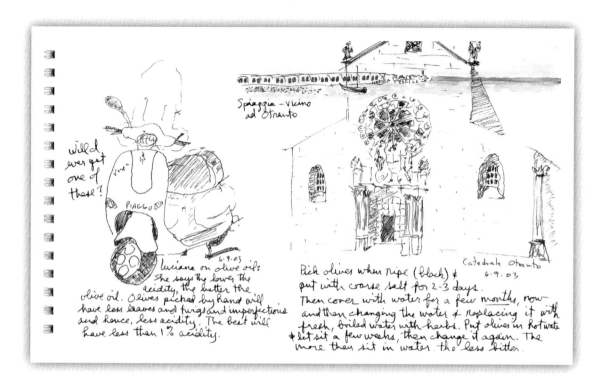

Will I ever get one of these?

PIAGGIO

6.9.03

Spiaggia – vicino ad Otranto

Cattedrale Otranto
6.9.03

Luciana on olive oil: She says the lower the acidity, the better the olive oil. Olives picked by hand will have less leaves and twigs and imperfections and hence, less acidity. The best will have less than 1% acidity.

Pick olives when ripe (black) & put with coarse salt for 2-3 days. Then cover with water for a few months, now and then changing the water & replacing it with fresh, boiled water with herbs. Put olives in hot water & let sit a few weeks, then change it again. The more they sit in water, the less bitter.

Medussa

Anise gone to seed

Our terrace ... Otranto. 9.28.05

Back to Otranto... the 5th year
Not a lot of changes. The tramontana is blowing, the temp. about 100°.
The water warm, but cloudy. We have a new coffee bar across from the
old Bar Centrale with the same great view of the Otranto Bay.
The apartment has a new canvas awning that brings welcome
shade, but a continuous flapping in the wind. ... we reconnect
with our Italian grocer - the young man who spends time in NYC.

Otranto 6.29.08

A morning conversation on the
beach after my swim with
a kindly gentleman who spoke
of his memories of Otranto. ...
"Domenico" worked as a prefect
throughout Italy, but was
born in Maglie and spent
his youth around Salento &
Otranto. Now he's retired and
spends time painting ceramics,
reading and writing ... also
surfing the internet. Wrote a
a letter to the editor published
in "Bel Paese" a local free
newspaper. Sees a great need
for transparency in government,
cooperation among interest groups.
... Also told the story of the
"Esther Williams Roll."

A steady stream of cement ships enter, load and leave
Otranto Harbor, bound for Albania ... In the distant
past, were they ships ladened with olive oil & wine?
Were they bound for Ithaca, Athens, Magna Grecia?
We hiked from the harbor, south, around a point,
along the rugged coast to a spot known to locals
as the "Orte." Oppressive heat of the morning sun,
rocky fields, sentinel tower, meadowlarks,
kestrels, magpies, and at the end of our hike, cool
clear swim in a cove filled with colorful fish and
underwater plants ... more swimming later in the day
in Otranto's harbor, escapes from the midday heat
— the water flat, unrippled, but cool of the Adriatic.

Otranto 7/6/08

7/7/08 — A drive over to the
Marina di Mancaversa — Carlo
& Lucia's summer destination
— Luccana's too. Lunch at
the trattoria "Menta e Rosmarino"
"Cucina Tipica". Seafood soup
with mussels, clams, crayfish,
shrimp and 2-3 kinds of
fish in a base of pomodorini,
prezzemolo, basil and fish
broth. Antipasti of melon
& prosciutto. Dessert of frozen
lemon — hollowed out and
filled with lemon gelato/sorbet.
Cold local white wine,
crusty toasted bread all
around a wide platter.
Caffé ... and oppressive
humidity! ... despite
the breezes off the Ionian
Sea.

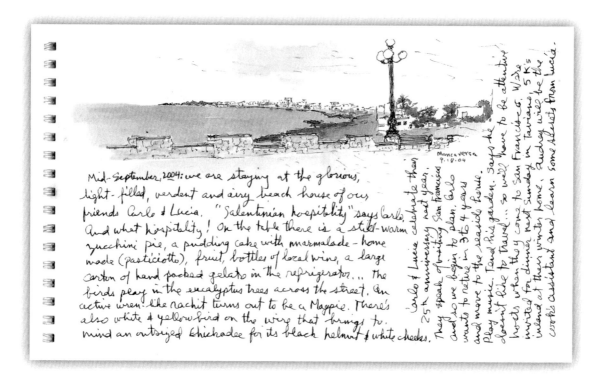

Mancaversa
9.18.04

Mid-September, 2004: we are staying at the glorious,
light-filled, verdant and airy beach house of our
friends Carlo & Lucia. "Salentinian hospitality" says Carlo.
And what hospitality! On the table there is a still-warm
zucchini pie, a pudding cake with marmalade - home
made (pasticiotto), fruit, bottles of local wine, a large
carton of hand packed gelato in the refrigerator... The
birds play in the eucalyptus trees across the street. An
active wren-like nachit turns out to be a Magpie. There's
also white & yellow bird on the wire that brings to
mind an outsized Chickadee for its black helmut & white cheeks.

Carlo & Lucia celebrate their
25th anniversary next year.
They speak of visiting San Francisco
and so we begin to plan. Carlo
wants to retire in 3 to 4 years
and move to the seaside home.
Play music. Tend his garden. Says he
doesn't like to travel ... so will have to be attentive
hosts when they come to San Francisco. We're
invited for dinner next Sunday in Taviano, 5 k's
inland at their winter home. Audrey will be the
cook's assistant and learn some secrets from Lucia.

Carlo & Lucia's
Seaside House in
Mancaversa
9/26/04

Mare
Mancaversa
9/26/04

Mancaversa is tranquil.
Down at the rocks, at each
end of the town, there is a
contingent of dedicated fishermen, each
with long pole and dangling line, always
rebaiting and, to the casual observer like me, never catching.
Dogs wander the streets. Short stubby things, but no one else. Then, at dusk,
the elderly couples (including me & Audrey) walk the boardwalk and watch
the sunset... getting the next days weather report.... rain & thunderstorms threaten...

Luciana's New house
7/1/13

We meet at 11:00 in the morning, pick up Carlo & Lucia in Mancaverse and head out to Luciana's garden and to see her new house. She's already there and has the place tidy and ready for her guests. We're first put to work... out in the field, picking cocomeri and zucchini, pulling a weed here and there. Then into the cool interior of her house for a cooking lesson and a work session on the book. Carlo takes me outside in the shade for a tamburello lesson... I'm rhythm challenged, but its my first lesson — he's had six months of lessons, so there is still hope. Next, we sit down for a snack and Luciana begins to bring out a series of dishes around the patronage know-how. Such wet sauce and Luciana's pasta... what she had prepared that morning. The conversation growing much she had prepared, food and recipes in flavors of she had the organic air, a reminder of Puliesia is a reminder of flavors the cool wind, and equally in Italy carried

"secolare" is the term for 100+ year-old olive trees. Salento is awash in them and we marvel at ulive (olive groves) of secolare — each twisted and gnarled tree with its unique personality. The trees are often numbered, each one kept track of and each ulive surrounded by "muri secche" (dry stone walls), often as old as the trees. It is against the law to disassemble the walls or remove an olive tree without a permit.

1/30/13
Spainzano, Salento

CHAPTER FOUR

Carlo

THE MUSIC MAKER

I became a true Salento citizen indirectly. What I mean is that usually if you are born in a given place, little by little, you grow up there, go to school, meet the people, appreciate the food, the landscape, the traditions, and the language until you realize you love living there and finally you feel and think you belong to the land and you are proud of it and you don't want to leave. This isn't exactly true for me.

When my mother became pregnant with me, she was in Sicily, having followed my father as good wives generally did in Italy in the 1940s. Though a Salentinian, he was assigned to Sicily as a soldier during the tragic post-war period when the island was about to fall prey to obscure conservative forces in a power struggle between the Mafia, secession supporters, and a few landowners on one side and the new-born democratic state on the other. There was a voluntary army called EVIS (Esercito Volontario per l'Indipendenza della Sicilia), whose main leader was Salvatore Giuliano, a well-known outlaw, set up and armed with the weapons of the former fascist army to fight against bringing the post-war democratic evolution in Italy. One of the results of the opposition to EVIS had been the victory of the left-wing parties in the 1947 local elections in Sicily. As a consequence, EVIS started storming police and Italian army barracks.

Two weeks before my birth, my mother decided I should be born in Salento, far from terrorist attacks, bombs, and rifle shots. She took the train and went back to her birthplace. So I was born in Salento as a war child.

A few years later, my father was transferred to Liguria, a region in the north of Italy, where my family lived until I was fourteen before returning to live in Salento for good. But every summer up until 1964, I spent my school holidays, almost three months, in Salento, in the town of Taviano.

I can still remember the long travel from Albenga, where we lived on the coast of the Ligurian Sea, to Taviano, an inland Salento village nestled amongst rows of olive trees and surrounded by burned lands, *terre bruciate*, hemmed in with dry stone walls, beginning as the train approached the coastal city of Brindisi and continuing to the end of the line in Lecce. It was a sort of Wild West, a remote homeland to me, a boy used to living in the north of Italy in a block of flats with running water, a bathroom, gas stove, and electric appliances.

In Taviano, I stayed at my grandparents' house, where the main energy source in the 1950s was a huge fireplace for cooking, heating, and hot water. Clothes ironing was performed with a heavy metal container filled with embers. Our water for general use came from a well in the yard. Drinking water came from a fountain in the street located thirty meters from the house.

At that time, Albenga, my hometown, was a seaside resort in the northern province of Liguria. Also it was an early fruit and vegetable agricultural town with hundreds of greenhouses growing flowers, strawberries, asparagus, and peaches. It was also famous for its basil, considered the best for making pesto, the rich, green, basil-based sauce that originated in the area.

On the other hand, Taviano was a farm village whose countryside was tilled by day laborers working on large estates alongside proprietors who only owned small patches of land for growing vegetables for the family. The main farm products were vegetables, legumes, grapes, olives, tomatoes, and peppers. A popular myth said that the peppers, imported by the Arabs, were poisonous and would kill the whole population. But it was untrue. Peppers became one of the pillars of the Salento diet, proving that not even the Arabs were able to erase Salento from history!

Anyway, to a young boy, Taviano seemed at least twenty years backward compared to Albenga in northern Italy. So when the coach heading north to take me home was about to leave Taviano, I used to shout every time from onboard: "*Ciao, terroni!*", a derogatory name when used by northern Italians to describe southern Italians. It means something like dullards, louts, or peasants and is highly offensive. I was only an eight-year-old boy, so I didn't understand the seriousness of the insult. On the other hand, all my relatives and friends gathered by the train door to watch me leave and shouted, chorus-like, "*Ciao, polentone!*", an equally egregious term referring to northern Italians, which means "slowpoke." *Polentone*'s origin is traced to *polenta*, the thick porridge made with maize flour, a traditional food eaten mainly in northern Italy. It also means "polenta eaters," a strong insult. So the match was a draw.

Returning permanently to Taviano in the 1960s wasn't so bad. In the winter evenings I loved to wander around the village with my new school friends. In the streets lit by dim lamps we would follow the heavenly smells emerging from the *rosticcerie* (delis that also serve hot food) in the back of the butcher shops, sometimes accepting the silent invitation to come in.

On long iron spits in a high hearth with an enormous fire, the butcher's wife roasted a row of *gnommareddhi* (rolled veal stuffed with sweetmeats), the origin of the mouth-watering fragrance. The woman put them on a clean white marble surface and poured a small heap of salt from a white paper bag. People say that the aroma of coffee is unbeatable when it emerges from an Italian *caffettiera* (coffee pot), but when you taste it, it doesn't measure up to what you had expected. Not so with *gnommareddhi*. Their taste was exactly what their smell had promised. But more importantly, you had to eat them in the back of the butcher's shop, with no cutlery, simply dunking each roulade in salt, standing in the warm and cozy back room next to peasants and workers drinking strong red wine. And maybe you had to be a teenager, too, partaking of a secret, comforting slice of local adult life.

Perhaps this is where I began feeling myself a Salentinian in my heart of hearts. Such apparently negligible episodes of daily life in Taviano, coupled with my summer adventures living with my grandparents, contributed to my connection to the land and its people. And although my decision to study languages at the university in Naples took me away and abroad, I came back to Salento to stay forever.

Carlo says: *According to an old tradition in the town of Taviano, on Fridays and Saturdays at the butcher's shop on Via Castelforte, opposite the church of Beata Vergine Addolorata, you can taste and purchase roasted meat of all kinds, grilled on a charcoal stove while you wait. In addition to choosing your own rolls (*gnommareddhi*), sausages, or beefsteaks, you can ask the cook to tell you the secret of the marinade he uses. If the butcher cooperates, you are bound to astonish and impress your guests at your next home barbecue.*

BLUESALENTO: SALENTO BLUES

Why does my band, Bluesalento, play this strange kind of music called *pizzica*? The story of how it became part of my music is very interesting, but please be warned, it is an especially long story.

A Song from the Past

In 1980, I worked as a teacher in a secondary school in a small town south of Lecce called Taurisano. It was the end of the term so the girls—it was an all-girls school—had organized a show. The hall was full of people: parents, relatives, teachers, and students. The atmosphere was merry and a bit noisy too.

Between the performances, unexpectedly, a voice was heard. A girl had started singing, causing the audience to break into silence. Her voice was pure and simple. The music sounded strangely ancient. The song was unknown to me, but at the same time, I knew it, as if it were a forgotten sound from my infancy. The lyrics said, "Women, oh women, going to work in the tobacco fields, two of you go and four come back." It's a riddle. Do you know what it means? The two women were made pregnant. That is how women were treated back then.

Eventually I realized the reason for the people's silence. The song the young girl sang spoke to all of us in the room. As a matter of fact, it was about us. It was the story of our great-grandmothers' labors, sufferings, and humiliations. The simple lines of the song echoed off the walls of the school hall, telling us how women were forced to live ages ago in Salento.

As a matter of fact, until the 1950s, in Salento and elsewhere in southern Italy the land was entirely in the hands of agricultural landowners who decided everything: which part of their land had to stay uncultivated, which part had to be turned over, which part had to be planted, and which peasants would be called to do the job. And in a period of hunger and dire poverty this meant they had the power to let people live or die by just giving one order.

For example, one day a landlord in Taviano decided to have one of his fields tilled, so he ordered his farm manager to take on twenty peasants from a list the manager had personally made. But at the dawn of the fixed day, twenty-five people stood in the field. The five extra workers, due to the extreme poverty of their families, asked the manager to let them work for at least that day's pay. In turn, the farm manager asked his master, who promptly called the *carabinieri* (the police) to report that the five poor people had invaded and occupied his field. The police were about to arrest the workers when a neighboring landowner, who had seen everything, felt pity for them and told the *carabinieri* that the five workers were there to till his own field. Later, my father told me the "good" landowner was one of my great-uncles.

Work, suffering, humiliation, salvation. What kind of music was this, so powerful in its re-creation of an entire age of history with just a few notes? And then it came to me: it was our ancestors' blues!

My Uncle Amedeo

A couple of years later, in May of 1982, I was at my father-in-law's house, along with one of his brothers, U Zzi Ameteu (Uncle Amedeo). The conversation was about their youth and the old times.

"Hey, Pippi, do you remember when we moved to Acquarica in 1934 and all the people used to say, 'Here come the Negroes,' because our skin had turned so dark after so many days walking around the countryside under the summer sun?"

"Of course, Ameteu! And after each walk not a single fig or prickly pear remained on the branches of the respective trees, to the annoyance of all the neighbors."

"I remember calculating the exact number of prickly pears I could eat before feeling sick."

And then, after a pause, as if they behaved this way often, they began singing a duet:

E bbeddha bbeddha te fice la toi mamma,   O beautiful girl, your momma made you,

E llu nome te lu mise la Matonna   and you were named after the Madonna

At that moment I surprised myself by joining in the chant as a third voice, adding to the harmony. The three of us together sounded like a human bagpipe. When the singing stopped, U Zzi Ameteu looked at me quite satisfied and said, "That's what people would call a pretty nice *cantu alla stisa.*"

Meanwhile, I wondered how I had managed to do that. I said to U Zzi, "I didn't even know the song."

"Are you kidding me?" asked Ameteu. "Of course you must know the song."

After a few days of reflection, I realized that Ameteu was right. I remembered those early morning songs from the summer of 1956, when my grandfather, a carter, whose work was to load the grape butts and carry them to the wine press, would take me with him to the vineyards. Along the country lanes, on the cart, in the dim light of dawn, I could hear the carters' voices, one after the other, singing that same song and many more. They did it to signal their positions in the area.

"My fellow travelers," they sang, "I'm here if you need me." Their voices were harsh, holding high, long notes so that they could be heard far away in the quiet of the fields.

The carters' songs had been hidden somewhere in my mind for such a long time that only that particular way of singing, *cantu alla stisa,* had managed to let them emerge. It translates into something like "music for unaccompanied voices." To be more exact, two main voices take the high and low notes, respectively, and the third voice swings around the middle notes, very much like a flute playing counterpoint, until the final prolonged verse. The swinging middle voice is the peculiar feature of the singing style of Salento. A fourth falsetto voice is often added, although it is not a rule. When you hear the songs, you realize that the vocal melody doesn't always follow the beat. It may speed up or slow down.

In fact, this way of singing is so ancient it was done without instruments. As my Uncle Ameteu would say, *minate ca nui secutamu* (start singing and we'll follow you), meaning that the song, usually very slow, was sort of a jam session of different voices, performed during and after the farm work. The role every singer took in the choir represented his or her individual and original contribution to the group. It was a social collaboration. And collaboration, at that time in our history, meant survival.

Therefore, although the first voice in the song often wasn't the best, it was the most confident and inspired the contributions of the other singers. While listening, they started singing one by one, each doing it in their own way. A really particular voice was the low one, the very basis of this music. It didn't sing the lyrics but provided the rhythm for the song, something like *umma-umma* or *maa-aa.* Every singer collaborated but each voice was different, in keeping with the individualism of the Salentinian character.

This individualistic character reminds me of another story. One day in the 1960s, some people from the labor unions came to Salento to recommend that the farmers create cooperatives in order to pile up the farm produce and sell it on better terms to the wholesalers. Apparently it was an idea that had worked well in northern Italy, but as it happened, not in Salento.

Thanks to a new law at that time, many farmers had purchased on easy credit their own patch of land from large agricultural estates, and for the first time in their lives they had become small landholders. Although the idea seemed to work for a few months, the trade unionists noticed that the number of members in each cooperative, instead of increasing, decreased day by day. When one of the outgoing farmers was asked the reason why, he replied, "You come here and claim that we should harvest our products on a precise date. But we have taken orders all our lives, and now for the first time we decide something on our own. So I want to pick my potatoes only when I smell something in the air telling me to do it, whether it's right or wrong. I want to sow the earth only after feeling and crumbling a clod of it from my field. I want to take my produce to the market myself and bargain with the wholesaler and have a cup of coffee with him after the negotiation. Does the Union understand this? I don't think so, and so I don't want to be a member."

A Taranta Night in Melpignano

In 1999 on a late summer evening, I went to a music festival in Melpignano, a village in the Grecia Salentina, an area in southern Salento where ancient Greek is still spoken. Several groups were performing on an outdoor stage. I was standing among hundreds of people listening to music. A young man came and stood in front of me. He wore glasses and a dark suit, a white-collar worker, as you say. On the stage, a tambourine player had started his beating, faster and faster, followed by the guitarist, alternating two simple chords. The rhythm became more and more obsessive. The man in front of me started shaking his shoulders up and down, then gradually his entire body, until I had to move backwards so as not to be hit by his rolling arms. In fact, he was now spinning around blindly, his eyes shut, his head swinging freely.

But as I watched him more carefully I realized that his movements were not completely free. He had a method. I recognized the steps of the dance. The people watching were familiar with it too. They made a circle around the young man, and someone nearby holding another tambourine started beating it in time with the rhythm of the band on the stage. He had the *taranta* spirit in his blood.

Carlo says: *If you go to Melpignano in the middle of August, you will have the opportunity to enjoy, along with more than 100,000 people from all over the world,* **La Notte della Taranta**. *It is the most important folk concert in Italy, performed by the orchestra with the same name, a large team of musicians playing both traditional instruments, such as tambourines, bagpipes, and mandolins, and classical instruments like guitars, violins, harps, and so on. Performers play and dance the* pizzica, *an ancient and frenzied form of movement and sound. It is a concert you will not forget.*
Info: www.lanottedellataranta.it

The Origins of *Taranta*

The very heart of *taranta* music is the tambourine or *tamburello* in Italian. It is the main instrument of the cure for what used to be an ancient disease. According to tradition, the peasants who worked in the fields harvesting wheat were often bitten by a local spider, a tarantula (*Lycosa tarantula*). Some of them would suddenly take ill, complaining of weakness, vomiting, and helplessness, having acquired "*taranta*." Nowadays, historians surmise that the real cause of the illness wasn't the tarantula bite but life itself. Poverty, hunger, oppression, and violence were the daily enemies of the rural population. And the weakest—mostly women—fell ill.

Since 100 AD, and even before, the remedy has been magic: the beat of the tambourine. Salento, a Greek-influenced land for centuries, has an "Eastern" culture. Greek vases in Salento museums show men holding tambourines, the same kind of tambourine that folk bands play today. Even the gestures are alike: the player holds the instrument upright with his left hand clenching the down side and beats the skin with his right hand. In Greek mythology Orpheus soothed wild beasts with the music of his lyre. Homer wrote about Greek heroes of Troy healed by music. In Salento, healers used tambourines, guitars, and violins to cure people of taranta. This music is called *pizzica* from the word *pizzicata*, the woman who has been bitten by the spider.

The Cure

As I have learned, the ancient pizzica has little to do with the popular pizzica music of today. Pizzica was created as a folk medicine for peasants. The players were invited to the sick woman's house to see her. After observing her blinking, they took the rhythm of her eyelids as the beat for their improvised song. The tambourine player, standing close to the sick woman's ear, started beating his instrument in order to build a percussive base.

You can hardly imagine the energy springing from a 15-inch-diameter tambourine beaten fast and strong. When my friend Sergio Lia beats it in a recording session, everything in the studio vibrates, and we have to hold the objects to stop them from echoing back. The effect of this rhythmic sound on the sick person was powerful. Her senses and psyche were strongly stimulated. The overload of aural sensations triggered a set of uncontrolled reactions: a woman followed the rhythm of the music by swinging her entire body. This was a sign that meant that the musicians had recognized the right kind of tarantula. If the woman, on the contrary, had remained restless, moaning and groaning in spite of the music, the players had to change the music until she reacted to the new rhythm by standing and dancing. She would then dance and dance so intensely and long that the tarantula tired and its spell was broken, finally leaving her alone and spent. This was the story of the tradition as my friend Sergio told it to me when we first met years ago.

Sergio Lia, the Tambourine Man

Sergio likes to talk about his tambourine. "I make my tambourines myself. I use different kinds of wood, such as cherry, olive, and acacia. I cut them and put them first in water to soak and then into a frame for a few days."

"Why don't you buy them in a music shop like everyone else?" I asked him.

"Because I'm not sure the one who made them is aware of the symbolism—yes, the symbols. The wood circle of the tambourine represents the harmony and perfection of the universe. It's connected to the shape of the sun and the planets and the spinning of the whole solar system. That's why the tambourine became the main instrument of the tarantula cure. It turned the irrationality of the disease back to the rational through its geometrical shape!"

Sergio, a young and handsome man in his mid-forties, lives in the countryside between the town of

Patù, only a few kilometers from the cape of Santa Maria di Leuca and the seaside village of San Gregorio, on the Ionian Sea. His house is set amongst olive trees and vineyards. In addition to tambourines, he makes his own olive oil and wine. Every year he picks the olives from the trees one by one, with care and love, because he has a lot of time and he's not interested in money. His oil is genuine and pure just as he is, a native Salentinian in love with simple, everyday things: a sunny morning in the fields, a *friseddha* (a slice of hard, crusty bread) with tomatoes, oil, and salt for lunch, a few friends at dinner drinking his homemade wine, laughing and playing music all night long.

"The tambourine shape is matched by the circle of people gathering around the dancing woman and the players during the 'cure,'" he continued. "Even the dancing figures turn in circles."

While he was talking, Sergio pressed the skin of the tambourine with his thumb, just to test its tension. The tambourine skin is fixed to the wood with pins made from his olive tree wood.

"This one," he said, "is made from a newborn lambskin—don't worry, it died a natural death."

Sergio continued, "So after recognizing what kind of tarantula had bitten the woman, she would be forced to dance to the sound of the pizzica for hours and hours, until the poison in her was broken down. Sometimes it would take a year of periodic dancing before the woman would be completely recovered."

The Salento Tambourine Technique

As we talked, he started beating the tambourine. This doesn't mean that he simply was beating the instrument with his open palm, as one imagines it is usually played. The local style is quite different, influencing the whole expression of this music. He wasn't striking the skin. He let his fingers hit it one by one by rolling his hand. In this technique, the fingers are stretched out and parallel to each other, and the thumb forms a sort of cylinder so that when the hand spins around, each finger strikes the skin rapidly and the beats are heard without interruption, like a hail of knocks. The first and strongest stroke is the one by the thumb, and it is placed at the beginning of the bar. In fact, this is only what you see, but the beating process is much more complex. It's made invisible by the speed of the hand flying on the instrument.

In order to give an account of the real beating process I decided, one day, to face the thing scientifically; that is, I started taking tambourine lessons so that I could test both the direct and indirect effects of playing the instrument. On the first day, my teacher came immediately to the point by showing me the basic movement of the percussion:

* The thumb bone gives a blow horizontally to the middle of the leather circle.

* The whole hand rotates right until the four fingers, lined up and slightly arched, touch the instrument with their fingertips.

* The fingers move up toward the upper part of the instrument.

* The hand then rotates left until the forefinger phalanx beats the tambourine rim.

* The four fingers next rotate right, touching the skin again with their tips.

* The fingers move down the middle of the instrument and then back to the beginning.

According to the rhythm of a medium-speed pizzica, the whole operation takes place in about one second, so it appears almost invisible to an ordinary observer. I believe no other technique in the world can produce such swift rhythms. Speed is the main reason why pizzica can become so intense and haunting.

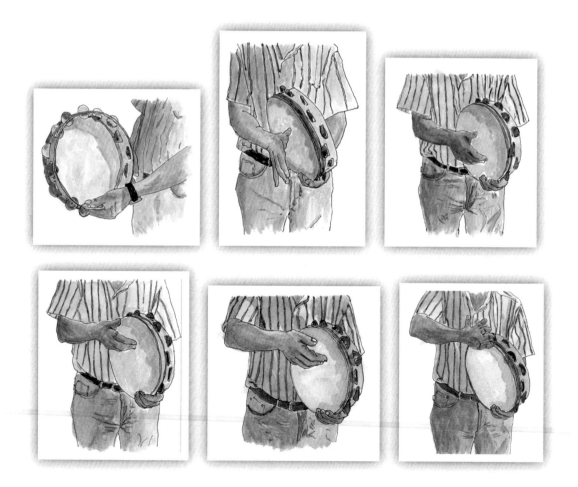

Sergio showed me another tambourine. "I made the rattles of this one from olive tree wood. The sound is different, not so harsh and shrill as with the traditional copper rattles we call *rami*."

The *rami* are a couple of copper discs fixed on the wooden circle of the tambourine. The instrument is moved up and down according to the rhythm of the song so that the rattles jingle. But, in fact, they are shaken with every single stroke on the skin, too. So their sound is extremely compounded.

The Musical Heritage of Salento

Little by little, I became aware of the immense musical legacy of Salento: hundreds of songs and lyrics, collected and organized by a handful of scholars in the 1950s and '60s. I was amazed at the amount and quality of the material. One of the main genres was the *moroloi*. The *moroloi*, descended from the old Greek *moira* (destiny) and *logos* (speech), are mourning chants—that is, singsong intonations rather than real songs. They are ancient. Some historians think the first ones were written years before Homer's *Iliad*. They were performed by professional singers whose job was to sit and cry and sing these *moroloi* during funerals. As part of the ritual, the singers held a white handkerchief and moved it rhythmically according to the song. The songs were composed of fixed lines of general meaning and a few improvised ones to fit the particular situation of the dead person and the family. Here is an example of what the women sang:

Te dhu viniu stu ientu refulu?   Where was this whirling wind from?
Ca quistu viniu te la marina   It was from the sea
E viniu a casa mia   And it came to my home
E nne spezzau la mejjiu cima   And broke the best branch

In addition, about a hundred love songs have been collected. I immediately appreciated the lyrics for their clarity and originality. On the other hand, some of them were medieval and resembled the Scuola Siciliana of poetry, where, for instance, a lover compares his woman to a "lady of the manor" or to a princess or a queen:

De sira ieu passai ppe nna padula   One night crossing a marsh
E ntisi le ranocchiule cantare   I heard the frogs singing

A una ieu le sintia cantare   One by one I heard them singing

Ca me pariane lu rusciu de lu mare   They seemed to me like the sound of the sea

Lu rusciu de lu mare é troppu forte   The sound of the sea is too loud

La fija de lu rre se dae la morte   The king's daughter takes her own life

Iddha alla morte e ieu alla vita   She is dead to me

La fija de lu rre se sta marita   The king's daughter is going to get married

Iddha se sta marita e ieu me nzuru   She's going to get married and I am, too

La fija te lu rre purtau nnu fiuru   The king's daughter brings a flower

Other songs are about desperate romances, such as this one with the lover in tears waiting night and day at his loved one's door, calling up death:

Chiangu miseru mie chiangu la sorte   I cry poor me, I complain of my fortune

Nun c'ete cchiu de mie nu spenturatu   no one else is so unlucky

Me facisse na 'isita la morte   I wish I could find my death

'nnanzi de l'alba o a matinu sunatu   before the dawn or in broad daylight

beddha ieu stau quaffore alle toi porte   Sweetheart, I'm standing outside your house

e sta spettu cu bessu giudecatu   waiting to be judged

Ci t'aggiu fatta qualche cosa 'n tortuif   I wronged you with anything

O le vecine m 'hannu murmuratuor   the neighborhood slandered me

Mo' giru tornu tornu le toi portenow   I keep walking past your house

Chiangendu la mia sorte e lu miu fatu   complaining of my lot and fate

But my favorite, owing to its delicacy and freshness, is the following:

Quannu te llai la facce la matina   Every time you wash your face in the morning

L'acqua ninella mia nu l'hai menare   little girl don't throw the water away

Ca ddhu la mini tie nasce la rosasince   where you pour it a rose grows

Na rosa e nu rusieddhu pe ndurarea   rose and a rosary to enjoy the smell

Ca ene lu speziale te la Cina   A chemist from China comes to me

Me face medicine pé sanare   makes medicines for me to recover

Mo pé sanare le ferite mei   in order to heal my wounds
Ca su d'amore e nu sananu maiyet   they are love wounds and won't ever recover

These songs make me remember, vaguely, as if in a dream, musicians playing in the streets at Christmastime when I was a small boy. They played the so-called *strina*, which means something like "Christmas present." Accordion, triangle, and snare drum players wandered the village singing the good news of the Redeemer's birth and the arrival of the shepherds and three kings in exchange for foodstuffs like eggs and cheese.

In fact, the *strina* is a set of Salentinian compositions that mark the beginning of the new year when adults can both sow their fields and reorient their lives. The songs have pagan roots, especially the ones performed in Grecia Salentina (the Greek villages). They were sung long before Christianity, although later on they were converted into religious chants announcing Christ's birth and the New Year. Here is an example:

Fermate amici miei no sciati Avanti   Stop, my friends, don't go ahead
Ca quai se fermane puru li venti   because here even the wind stops
Ca quai se fermane li soni i canti   because here the sounds and the chants stop
Ca pene no ci stannu ne lamenti   here are no sorrows, no moans

A quai io su 'rrivatu a quai me fermu   I came here and here I stop
'rretu le porte de ste case toeby   the door of your house
insieme agli strumenti noi cantiamo   we are singing with our instruments
e qualche verso a vostra signoria   and a few lyrics for you

Bon capudanno chi si fa la strina   Happy New Year to the ones who give presents
Come la fice Santu Silvestruas   Saint Sylvester did
Ca li re Maggi l'hannu fatta prima   And the Magi did before him
Ci l'hannu 'ndutta a 'stu mundu diversu   Making this world so unique

At Easter, the Passion was also a musical event performed by two singers accompanied by an accordion, singing alternate verses, describing Christ's trials, his condemnation, the burden of the cross, and the crucifixion. It was a complex ceremony, involving the transport of an olive branch from one village to the next, where it was ritually planted at the performance site. Once, during the singing, in the Salento town of Martano, I saw women identifying with the Madonna as they burst into tears upon hearing the following line: "... *la Madonna sintennu ste palore tutti li carni soi se vò strazzare*" (... the Madonna hearing these words wanted to tear all her flesh). And even old men trembled with emotion.

The Turnaround

How far away my very own blues band was from all of this ancient Salentine music! How did that happen? What were the reasons my generation of local musicians had completely disregarded their musical roots and turned to the sound of modern rock and blues—obviously great music but music descended from a different cultural milieu, one that we Salentinians had no connection to.

One night I was talking with Luigi Liotta, the lead guitarist of our musical group, Bluesalento. It was late and we were in the recording studio.

"Luigi," I said, "we can appreciate these blues songs, we can admire the artists, we can go to concerts to listen to them, but how can we play only this kind of music our whole lives? We have some responsibility to honor our forefathers' culture and music, don't you think? It's our heritage."

Let me explain further. Luigi is a fantastic blues player. At his best, he can make his guitar do whatever he wants: cry, laugh, fly like a helicopter and whiz like a rocket at the same time. He has been playing guitar since he was fourteen. In the early times he didn't have a guitar of his own. His passion for the music forced him to borrow instruments here and there continuously. He owned an old record player and listened to the same musical passages he was interested in over and over until the record was ruined, just so he could reproduce it on the guitar. His friends say that once, in a burst of sudden anger and frustration, unable to reproduce what he had heard on the record, he punched his borrowed guitar, opening a hole on its upper side. When he returned the guitar to its horrified owner, he apologized, saying that he was sorry but the guitar was a wild beast that refused to obey him.

I can't count the numerous hours Luigi has spent perfecting his musical style; the many mornings he was truant from school to attend the rehearsals of The Killers, one of the first rock groups in Salento; the nights he spent playing the blues down in a damp, dark cellar with musicians who were unable to understand what real blues music was like.

He had been a bluesman for years. He had been talking like a bluesman. He had been thinking, feeling, and dreaming like a bluesman. And now, here I was, asking him to radically change his way of playing—to change his philosophy and his way of living and viewing the world. I expected him to be angry and puzzled.

But that night in the studio he looked at me and said, very quietly, "A few years ago, I recorded my grandparents singing several *canti alla stisa*. I've got them on tape. We could start listening to them. They are really fabulous."

He proceeded to tell me that recently he had gone to Santa Cesarea Terme, a small coastal town on the Adriatic, where his grandparents were staying for two weeks at a health spa. In their hotel room, he had placed two microphones and his tape recorder while his grandma called in some of the guests at the hotel, all of them people in their seventies and older. Each one in the group, owing to a sort of innate knowledge, spontaneously chose a certain place to stand in the room. The high voices stood in the middle and the low voices along the sides.

Carlo says: *At the town of Santa Cesarea, on the Adriatic coast south of Otranto, the waters of hot sulfur springs emerge in four caves. These waters have served as a health cure for hundreds of years. According to one legend, the springs gushed from the remains of a group of giants killed by Hercules. Another legend tells of a maid called Cisaria who sheltered in one of the caves to escape her father. Whatever the case, you can soak in the waters as treatment for respiratory diseases, skin diseases, and more. At the same time, the waters are delightful for just relaxing.*
Info: www.termesantacesarea.it/

A lively elderly lady, trying to organize the improvised choir while at the same time reproaching her husband, a man in his eighties, for being unable to sing properly, attracted Luigi's attention. Her name was Tottò and she was well known as the owner of a grocery store open year round in the seaside village of Mancaversa. That night in the hotel room, Luigi explained, she gathered all her old friends together to perform a series of *canti alla stisa* for Luigi's tape recorder.

"La Cerva" (The Doe) is one of the most interesting that Luigi recorded:

Nnu ggiurnu andai a ccaccia alla foresta   One day I went hunting in the forest
Intra llu bboscu de Ninella miain   my Ninella's wood
Viddi nna cerva e lli truncai la testa   I saw a doe and I beheaded it
Morta nu bbera e llu sangu scurria   It was still alive and its blood was running
Se nfaccia la patruna de la finestra   My lady appeared at the window

Non ammazzà la cerva ca è la mia   Don't kill the doe because it's mine
No ssu bbinutu pè mmazzà la cerva   I haven't come to kill the doe
Jeu su bbinutu per amare a ttia   I have come to love you

And so together we began our work with ancient Salentinian music. At first we just analyzed the recorded items, trying to understand their inner structure, the way they had been imagined and written, the settings where they were played day by day. Luigi was there with me. His interest and support both surprised and relieved me at the same time. He was my best friend. Our life-long friendship was based on our mutual, strong love for music. I would not have been able to go in a different direction without him.

Sooner or later we had to tell the rest of the group what we had decided. They reacted without saying a single word. They put their instruments into their cases and carried them out of the studio and disappeared. The bass player turned his head while walking away and said, "I had been told you were completely crazy but I didn't believe it. Now I know they were right. I'll tell you just one thing—you will never get out of this cellar with the stuff you're going to play now."

The door slammed on us, echoing for ten seconds in the silence. We were no longer a group, just a pair of desperate, lonely musicians from southern Salento. Now we needed a new drummer and keyboard player as well as a bass man. Everyone in the music business around us was only a rock-blues-gospel-jazz-samba player. We felt like pilgrims crossing a desert full of hostile strangers, speaking any language but our own. The paradox was that we were trueborn people from Salento, asking only to sing and play authentic music from our land! We realized how strong and powerful the global music machine had been, coming along with mighty advertising campaigns, thousands of songs broadcast by every radio in the country, every movie house, internet videos, and so forth. We felt that we were facing the risk of disappearing as a singing people, replaced by a one-dimensional brave new world of homogenized music.

We wrote an article and sent it to *La Voce*, a local newspaper printed in our town of Taviano but popular in the whole area. It was an appeal for a "revival" of the ethnic music of Salento. We argued that so much of the music played in the world had its origins in the popular traditions of each country, arranged and stylized by local artists, yet in Salento, this process had not yet taken place. The continuity of our traditional music had been interrupted, like a broken piece of a Darwinian chain, owing perhaps to the invasion of foreign cultural influences. So we wrote that it was our duty as local musicians to restart the blossoming and to give full expression to our forefathers' musical heritage. The article was received favorably. Several musicians called us. In two weeks' time, we started playing with a brand new Bluesalento. Bluesalento's stage is now a meeting place for different kinds of traditional musicians, singers, actors, and dancers, both classical and modern. We are proud that our musical performances now represent the rich, complex, and ever-evolving Salentinian culture.

A DAY ON THE ROCKS

The enormous cliff, dark as a mountain, towered over a five-year-old boy floating precariously in the wild Salento sea. Crabs with tiny, hostile eyes, round and black like peppercorns, scuttled on the rock half a meter away from a rubber gosling holding the child afloat. Sand hoppers crawled among the cliff moss and seaweed while a whitish blob roamed along the green seafloor. A sudden wave drove the child into a crevice in the cliff where an unknown sea monster's frightening jaw waited to snatch the boy. He screamed. He was a city boy, used to a calm summer sea, Italian bathing establishments with small beach tents lined up in a reassuring order, and soft, level sand beneath his feet.

"Grab that boy!" cried my aunt Lina from the top of the cliff to my cousin Adele. With a couple of easy strokes, she dragged me out of the crevice until I hugged a nearby rock, a safe place, and scrambled quickly up and onto the edge of the steep cliff next to my aunt. From there, I watched Adele, a tall and sturdy young woman in her twenties, swim and sing lightheartedly amongst crabs, octopuses, seaweed, urchins, and other unknown horrible floating creatures.

"Not me," I said to myself. "No more swimming in this wild sea! One must be crazy to go bathing here! Never again!"

Of course, as I grew older and as summers came and went I was destined to change my mind, but I can still feel the terrible fear I experienced that day. I found it comforting to learn that there was a Salento proverb, *"Mare viti e ffussci; taverna viti e trasi,"* meaning "If you see the sea, take to your heels; if you see a tavern, go in." I wasn't the only one afraid of the sea.

All the people of Salento were once afraid of the sea, though owing to reasons quite different from mine. First of all, until relatively recently, the coasts had been marshy for centuries. This meant unhealthy places infested with scorpions, snakes, spiders, and malarial mosquitoes and, above all, land that was not cultivable. So people stayed away from the shores and the sea. But there was another, more important reason: pirates. Ever since the Turks had conquered Constantinople in 1453 and Otranto in 1480, their sailing ships had appeared on the open sea along the coasts to raid the villages. The dreaded pirates had to be sighted well in advance to give the peasants time to flee inland, taking their few belongings with them. To do so, many watchtowers were built along the Salento coast, one every five kilometers. About sixty are still there, almost intact, forming a necklace around the peninsula. For centuries, danger had come from the sea, therefore, "Sea: see and take to your heels." Nowadays, several seaside villages in Salento take their name from a tower, such as Torre Suda, Torre Vado, Torre San Giovanni, Torre Chianca, and so on.

This entire area is only knee deep... we walk to islands & try to swim in the reed.

Porto Cesareo
7·21·03

Torre Lapillo

After coming of age, I changed my mind about the sea, as I realized how different the Salento Sea in southern Italy was from the Ligurian Sea next to my hometown of Albenga, in northwestern Italy. The Ligurian Sea was gray or brown and rough most of the time, becoming calm for only a few days during the summer when, like a miracle, it transformed itself into a shimmery light blue that was both warm and still. The beaches in the north were sandy, though the grayish and slightly dusty sand was brought in each spring by trucks from the nearest quarry. A meter from the water's edge, the sand gave way to large, uneven rocks that hurt my feet. When I entered the water to swim, I found myself surrounded by cigarette stubs, random seaweed, and pieces of wood and waste, the leftover detritus of rough seas.

In the south, on the other hand, where the Ionian Sea meets the Salento Peninsula and where I often spent my summers visiting my grandparents, the sea was typically green and transparent. It was a live body of water that smelled fresh and clean and contained healthy, natural marine plants and iodine.

One of my strongest memories of growing up next to the Salentinian sea happened one typically warm summer day when my high school friends and I camped near the cliffs on the Salento coast. There was no one around for kilometers. We were at a place called Pizzo, which means "promontory." It was situated a few kilometers south of the town of Gallipoli on a spit of land that later became a protected park, owing to a rare breed of tiny orchid that grows there on the sandy dunes along with evergreen bushes and herbal plants. It was a perfect place for a picnic.

My friend Mario, the best swimmer and diver of our group, made us all a bet: "I'll catch so many fish that you won't be able to eat them all, and you'll beg me to stop. Until you stop me, I'll go on fishing." He pointed to his backpack and said, "I have a pan and a bottle of olive oil to fry them in."

Mario was a thickset, strong seventeen-year-old with a head of curly hair. In spite of his formidable appearance, he was sweet and quiet. And he had the distinctive character trait that made him feel at ease only in the sea. He did not regard swimming in the sea in summer as a way to cool off or as exercise; instead, he preferred to fish. He would cast his line in both spring and fall and was content with the silence of the deep sea. Even when he returned without fish he would smile and seem satisfied. Yet as much as he loved fishing with a pole, his greatest pleasure was to dive underwater for the seafood bounty he could bring up from the depths.

So on that summer day at Pizzo, Mario began to fish. The first time he dove beneath the surface, he came up with a hundred or more sea urchins in his net. Sea urchins are strange creatures. It is hard to imagine that inside a black, thorny shell one can find tiny, tasty, crown-shaped, yellow and orange eggs. The challenge for the inexperienced is how to get at the precious eggs since the spines are so sharp and prickly.

The secret is to put the urchin in the palm of your hand with the spines facing downward. Not unlike walking on a bed of nails, the more nails there are, the less they penetrate. Holding the urchin in this way, you can then put a knife into its soft muzzle and lever it up to uncover the eggs. Of course, the best part follows: scoop the eggs out with a teaspoon to taste and savor the pure delight. Or, even better, double the pleasure of this blissful taste by using your tongue instead of a spoon.

As it turns out, sea urchins are male chauvinists, of a sort. In ancient Italian society, men were the only acceptable breadwinners and official producers of goods. From a biological point of view, the urchins bearing the eggs are, obviously, the females, but in our Salentinian dialect they are called *masculi*, meaning "males." Men refused to recognize that female sea creatures could make such a delicacy, and the result was that male supremacy won out.

ricci

That day on the rocks, we ate the urchins. The scene was a ballet of sorts: we, the dancers, staggered over uneven rocks as we went to and fro along the water's edge, bending down to wash the open shells from impurities before savoring them. The strange dances went on about half an hour, time enough to eat about a hundred urchins, pleasurable each time our tongues touched the orange crown of the eggs and painful when a spine punished our greed.

Mario, swimming just offshore, checked to see if we were still busy with our meal. If we had nothing to eat, we would make fun of him.

We had just finished the last urchin when we noticed that Mario had caught three octopuses—or rather the octopuses had caught him. He emerged from the sea with the still-alive animals stuck by their suckers to his chest and arms, like living tattoos.

"Once I have seen it, the octopus is mine," he boasted, acknowledging the difficulty in spotting an octopus underwater before it sees you and transforms itself through camouflage into looking like a cliff or a piece of sea coral. "If it sees you first, the octopus will duck into a hole and disappear," he explained. As soon as he had seen this octopus, he had sprayed it with a light sulfur solution. The irritated animal came out of its hole and clung to his arm. Caught! Boasting, he displayed the little red suction circles left by the octopus.

Minutes later, Mario surfaced again with two groupers on his harpoon. He remained ashore just long enough to show us how to gut a grouper with a knife. Holding the head of the fish, he sank the triangular blade into its abdomen, letting the entrails drop to the water's edge. "Good for the crabs!" he said. "Now go on like that with the other one." We looked at each other in despair, waiting for the one of us brave enough to do the operation.

"Come on, I'll do it," I said finally. It wasn't my favorite job, but I had become more and more hungry after the urchin appetizers and had realized it was the only opportunity to have a proper lunch, sitting there in the wild, seven kilometers from home and a long way from the nearest snack bar. So I did the deed in silence. After all, I was feeding not only the crabs but also the seagulls, floating above with their wings open, hovering in the south wind.

With octopus and grouper, it was time to light a fire. We gathered bush twigs and herbs from cliff crevices: rosemary, thyme, cistus, lentisk, and myrtle. We selected dried branches already withered, and when lit, they immediately caught fire and gave off spirals of aromatic smoke. The hot oil sizzled in the pan as we fried and ate the fish, tasty with salt from seawater. It was hard to imagine that only five minutes earlier they had been alive and swimming.

But there's another kind of taste in the Salento sea. It is the subtle merging of tangy sweetness of air with the seawater, the dry dust of the yellow cliffs and the odiferous marine herbs that grow amongst the crabs, mussels, and shellfish. The aroma that comes from the sea is the gas given off by the phytoplankton, tiny bacteria-like creatures that inhabit the sea and serve as the foundation for the sea's food chain. Salentinians say that the taste and smell "get into your bones"—*te trase intr'a ll'osse*.

Carlo says: Lido Pizzo *is the only beach in Salento inside a wildlife reserve, called* **Isola di Sant'Andrea-Punta Pizzo**. *It is four kilometers (two and a half miles) south of Gallipoli. You will find white sands, a blue, crystal-clear sea, and a grove of pine trees. The restaurant on the beach serves delicious seafood.* Info: www.lidopizzo.it/

Our appetites were not yet satisfied so Mario continued fishing, and we continued eating until finally, after devouring a small school of red mullets, Mario had won the bet, and we begged him to stop and have mercy on us. Full and drowsy, we lay half asleep on the least uneven rocks. I realized Mario hadn't eaten a single bite.

"There's still some fish in the pan. Why don't you taste it?" I asked.

"I don't like fish. I prefer a good steak," he said. I still don't know if he was joking or being serious. I ought to have asked him at the time, but I didn't. I was too sated and lost in my own thoughts of the sea.

Years later, long after we had gone separate ways in our lives, I learned that Mario had died in his forties of a heart attack, at sea in his fishing boat. I like to think he is lying comfortably on the ocean floor, embraced by marine plants, his cheek on a soft sand pillow, smiling as if in a dream, waking only to fish.

underwater view of *ricci*

OCTOPUS COOKED IN A TERRA-COTTA POT

Polipo alla pignata

Octopus is easily found throughout Salento wherever fish are sold. In the States, at least in California, if we can find it at all, we often have to pre-order and buy it frozen. After eating this homemade dish with our Italian friends, Lucia gave us this recipe so that we could make it in our Otranto apartment. "Buy it cleaned and ready to cook," she said. "You can even have the fish seller cut it up for you." The terra-cotta cooking pot, called a *pignata*, is sold in markets throughout Italy and can be found in most cookware shops in the States. It can be used on top of the stove or in the oven. It is important that the octopus cooks in its own juices, so keep the lid on tight. This recipe serves 4.

Ingredients:
2 lbs octopus (one large or 2 smallish octopuses), cleaned and cut into small pieces (eyes, snout, and brain material removed)
2 cups tomato sauce
1 large onion, chopped
3 bay leaves
6–7 tbsp olive oil
½ cup parsley, chopped
Small handful of peppercorns
Pinch of salt
Crushed red pepper to taste (optional)

Add olive oil, chopped onion, tomato sauce, bay leaves, chopped parsley, peppercorns, and pinch of salt to the terra-cotta pot.

Cover and cook for 10 minutes.

Add the cleaned and cut octopus to the pot.

Cover tightly with lid and cook over a low heat (or in a 250 degree Fahrenheit oven) for about 2 hours.

Do not add water while cooking, and do not let vapor out of the pot as it boils; you may want to place a weight on the lid to keep it sealed.

Lucia says that when the pot starts making popping sounds, the octopus is ready to eat. Serve with homemade croutons.

TAVIANESI VS. RACALINI

The people who live in the approximately one hundred towns of Salento have much in common but the differences are what catch my attention. Take, for example, my hometown of Taviano, situated only a couple of kilometers from another smallish town, Racale. I can recognize a person from Racale just by listening to him talk for ten seconds. Why? Because of the variation in the dialect. In Italy, not only are there many dialects but also variations within the dialects. Taken all together, the differences are so many that no article, essay, book, or encyclopedia could cover them all. But let me give you more examples of how the two towns are different.

Take this ancient saying in the Salento dialect: *racalini occhi cacati*, meaning "the people of Racale have scabs in their eyes and granular lids." Racale citizens, suffering from drought, were unable to grow vegetables and consequently developed a vitamin deficiency that caused trachoma, an eye disease evidenced by granular lids. Meanwhile, the people of Taviano were said to have bloated stomachs because of malaria, "*tajanesi ventri nchiati*" in dialect. Long ago, all the water of the valley converged in almost impermeable basins to form marshes and bogs surrounding Taviano. Mosquitoes spread malaria in the town. Today, the marshes have been drained, and malaria has been eradicated, but the stigma of bloated stomachs persists.

These two towns, Taviano and Racale, so near each other but with differing geography and illnesses, also developed reputations for unique cultural talents. A local saying, "*racalini sonatori, tajanesi tintori*," says that the Racalini are good musicians while the Tavianesi are good painters. Present-day visitors and locals notice that Racale's children are charmed by any sound, while children from Taviano are fond of shapes and colors. No one can explain this but the belief exists.

What do Taviano and Racale have in common? As inland towns, they share a common relationship with seaside towns, mainly Gallipoli, twelve kilometers away on the Ionian coast. Until recently, the fishermen from Gallipoli used to sail southward with their rowboats and lower their fishing nets in front of Mancaversa and Torre Suda, the seaside resorts for Taviano and Racale. The fishermen's work lasted many days, and at night, instead of sailing back to Gallipoli, they slept on the beaches. The beaches became huge bartering sites, where the fishermen were greedy for the vegetables grown in the inland areas, while the inhabitants of Taviano and Racale needed fish. Traders from Gallipoli often visited the inland towns in search of vegetables or eggs in exchange for fish, though these relationships weren't always cordial.

The inhabitants of Gallipoli, sea people, thought highly of themselves and called people from

Taviano "*poppiti*" (big feet) because they tilled the land with their bare and muddy feet. The origin of *poppiti*, a word used throughout Salento, comes from the Latin *ob oppudom*, meaning "outside of town," therefore, peasant or uneducated person. However, the people from Gallipoli greatly appreciated the quality of the wine and the olive oil coming from the work of those "poppiti"—so much so that they couldn't have managed without them.

Another kind of rivalry that was most remarkable was between peasants and carters in Salento. The peasant land culture was dominant as the real producer of material goods, whereas the carter's job was essential for the transport of the produce. As a result, we had individuals with very different tempers. For centuries the peasant had been a tenant farmer tilling soil owned by others, so he was subject to a master and behaved as a servant. On the contrary, the carter was an independent worker freely serving those who called him, so he had an exuberant, even provocative temper, with a strong physique so as to be able to manage delicate or dangerous loads and uneven paths or deal with his cart and horse while crossing hills or canals. The peasant was fatalistic, used to bowing down to insolent owners and unfavorable weather and, therefore, more thoughtful and patient, unlike the impetuous and hasty nature of the carter. That's why peasants insulted their workmates by saying "*Zzappi mancu nnu travinieri!*" You're hoeing worse than a carter! And the carters, in return, replied, "You tied this knot worse than a peasant!"

And strangely enough, today the rivalry between the north and south of Italy is reproduced in miniature in Salento, though in a funny way. Generally speaking, northern Salentinians consider southern Salentinians a bit backward or uncouth or coarse, calling them "the ones living in the cape." The amusing thing is that because there are no borders, the people from Lecce, a central, inland city, consider "*capu*" (cape) to be all the towns south of it to the end of the Salentine Peninsula. But then, in turn, each town southward does the same to the next town, demonstrating this movable concept. People in Gallipoli and Taviano think the cape starts from Ugento, people from Ugento think it starts from Acquarica, and so on, until one reaches Santa Maria di Leuca, the town situated at the end of the peninsula. Its inhabitants can't deny that they live at the cape because now there's no more land, only the sea! Contrary to the idea that the farther south one travels, the rougher the people become, Santa Maria di Leuca is filled with old majestic villas facing the sea and the gracious Italians who inhabit them.

Santa Maria di Leuca

THE SAINTS COME MARCHING

An Italian marching band is usually a small to large group of musicians who play wind instruments and follow the local saint's celebratory procession. The first "official" band of Salento was founded in 1940 in the town of Racale. Every town has a festival with a band at least twice a year since each town has at least two patron saints. So there is music and celebratory fireworks throughout the year in Salento. After the procession, the band plays for the people beneath a bandstand generally placed in the main square. The wooden bandstand, painted in white, is made of a shallow dome held up by slim neoclassical columns. Under this pretty roof, the band plays the most famous arias, generally by Italian composers, such as Rossini, Verdi, Mascagni, Ponchielli, or Puccini, and often sung by skillful tenors and sopranos. The title of each piece appears on a wooden revolving sheet next to the stage. Moreover, the square is illuminated. This is a heritage from the Spanish domination of southern Italy in the seventeenth century. Thousands of bulbs (before electricity they were lit candles) are placed on large wooden frames shaped to imitate the façade of a baroque church and interlocked with a delicacy that resembles aerial lace.

In Salento, there is no celebration without *scapece* (tiny sardines rolled in flour and fried, set down in layers of breadcrumbs soaked with white vinegar and infused with saffron), the typical food of festivals, sold in the streets in big tubs. This fragrant food is yellow (from the saffron) and symbolizes the loud, triumphal, religious celebration of the town saint.

The Saint's procession and that of Good Friday were once unique, spectacular, and complicated ceremonies, beginning with a mobile canopy supported by four poles held by clerics to protect the holy symbol of God. Each priest walked with a cleric next to him, holding a mystical umbrella of liturgically-colored cloth designed to protect the celebrant, followed by the religious brotherhoods, each one wearing its own unique and colorful uniform and carrying a crucifix. The young candidates for confirmation walked alongside, dressed as pages with corduroy trousers, plumed, wide-brimmed caps, and silver dress swords, representing symbolic knights defending Jesus Christ's faith, according to ancient Spanish tradition.

Nowadays, everything is much simpler, yet many people still follow the statue of the saint. During the Corpus Christi procession, all the families who live along the route display beautiful plants, flowers, embroidered cloths, and small lights. It is not always flowers and plants. Once, during a long period of drought, a peasant put a salted sardine into the mouth of Saint Martin's statue so that the saint would realize how much the countryside needed water.

Another story tells of a farmer who, after following the statue in the procession, asked Saint Martin to answer a prayer by crying out, "*Te canuscu pirazzu*!" which translates to "I knew you as a wild pear tree!" The man meant he had been acquainted with the statue (and the saint) since it had been carved from the wood of his own pear tree. How could the saint refuse this man his holy support in the face of such truth? How comfortable the farmer was in confronting his patron saint! Today, the saying is used frequently to mean, "Don't tell me lies about your childhood, *te canuscu pirazzu*" (I've known you too long) or "You may now be a well-known lawyer, but *te canuscu pirazzu*" (I knew you when . . .).

Carlo says: *For more local culture, visit Taviano's* **Associazione Culturale "Vittorio Bachelet,"** *on Via Immacolata, a dynamic, creative, and prolific club that arranges book readings, concerts, comedy, films, or a mix of these every week or so.*

Carlo says: *In Taviano's historical center, on Via Immacolata, you will find the bookstore* **Libreria Antica Roma**, *with books on the ground floor, readings and lectures upstairs.*

JEWELS: L'ACCHIATURA

In order to understand how L'Acchiatura, a restaurant in Racale, is so different from any other restaurant in Salento, you have to go there. The mystery of the place begins with the name. It means "a chest full of jewels and valuables." The legend goes that if you are lucky, really lucky, just once in your life you will meet a *scazzamurrieddhu*, a Salentinian elf who can reveal the place where the *acchiatura* is buried.

It is said that a man from Taviano was told by an elf about a precious casket buried under the altar in Santa Marina church, an ancient place along the old road to Mancaversa by the sea. No one knows the lucky man's name or whether he really found the treasure, but according to the legend, the *scazzamurrieddhu* who led him to the treasure became a lifelong pest.

My father told me that one time a family was forced to move from their home in order to escape from one of these pestiferous elves. On the way to their new house, the mother asked the rest of the family if they had removed everything from the old house. One of the children cried out, "Oh dear! We forgot the broom!" But soon after, they heard the *scazzamurreddhu*'s voice saying, "Don't worry, here it is! I have brought it to the new house myself." That's how difficult it was to escape from it.

But when we entered the restaurant L' Acchiatura with our North American guests, elves were nowhere to be seen. We passed through a labyrinth of small and large rooms, each one with a perfectly set table that fit the size of the room. The inside garden is a small citrus grove. We sat at a table very close to the coolness of the lemon garden. In front of us was a wall made of bare ancient bricks, a 1000-year-old relic. We were dining in a medieval palace called Palazzo Briganti, built in the tenth century.

Carlo says: *L'Acchiatura's walls still hold two precious frescoes: a fourteenth-century Madonna and a seventeenth-century Christ. In the same neighborhood, don't miss the Ducal Palace with its two towers and the Church of Saint Mary of Heaven, dating back to the eleventh century, both rich in medieval mystery.* Info: www.acchiatura.it/

Carlo says: *Another special restaurant in Taviano is* **Vico degli Scettici** *(Alley of the Skeptics), on Via Matterotti, 14, in a restored Salento house with vaulted ceilings, rough walls, and a small theater for live plays and music. In the summer you can dine on the terrace overlooking the rooftops of Taviano.*

A real waiter, not an elf, surprised us. He served us a large number of traditional appetizers: *taraddhi mari* (ring-shaped salted crackers), *pucce* (tomato and olive bread rolls), *pittule culla burraccia* (fritters with borage), *cucuzzieddhi alla menta* (zucchini with mint), *caulifiuri fritti* (fried cauliflower), *pitta di patate* (potato cakes), *maranciane buttunate* (baked eggplant with tomato sauce), *sanapi e alici* (anchovies with black mustard), along with a cold and fragrant rosé wine.

When it was time to order more food, he asked, "What about a magnificent *purpu alla pignata*?" His elf-waiter voice was seductive. There was a bit of magic about him since he was a fluent English speaker, which isn't very common in Salento. He was not shy about revealing the ingredients of this typical Salentinian recipe: the octopus, after cutting it into pieces, is cooked in a terra-cotta pot with olive oil, tomato sauce, bay leaves, chopped onion, salt, and crushed red pepper. That's all, but watch out—there's a secret. He looked around slowly, as if he were afraid someone could hear his words. Then he bent over us and whispered, "*Lu purpu se coce cull'acqua sua stessa*," an ancient saying that means that the octopus cooks in its own fluids. "No water is added, a top is put on the pot with a weight to hold it down. And one should not remove the top until it is time."

Someone asked, "How do we know when it's time?"

"Exactly when the pot starts popping!"

The waiter continued, "I knew the beast personally. Last night it was still tossing in front of its lair on the seafloor, and I was above in my boat, fishing by lamplight."

Sounding a bit like Captain Ahab, he continued with his telling of the tale.

"The octopus was a bit dazzled by my light, but it looked as if it had the situation in hand." He said hand instead of tentacles, but we all kept silent.

"And just at the right moment, I dropped this."

He pulled out a rusty metal wedge with several hooks fixed to its base along with a remnant of white material.

"The material flutters under the sea and makes the octopus curious. But this one was cunning and just brushed my wedge with a tentacle. So I slowly moved the thing away from it and . . . suddenly the octopus jumped on the bait and hugged it with its entire body!"

He walked slowly around our table and ended his story with a triumphant smile. "I've little left to say except I just gave the wedge a tug and caught the beast."

Later, after we had sampled the cooked octopus, he said, "I suppose you noticed how the octopus was tender . . . there are a few operations that are done to get this result: first, when you are still on the boat with the beast alive next to you, you have to kill it at once, because it always tries to attack you with its suckers. This is not good for your skin. You kill the octopus by simply biting its head between the eyes. It is dead in a moment. Then, when you reach land, you take the octopus and bang it several times against a rock in order to kill its nerve endings. Finally, you rub it on a flat, rough stone for a few minutes, and now the animal is ready to be cooked!"

There was more. Another surprise was in store for us. Our waiter announced, "We've got only one kind of dessert. It's called *sporcamusi*, phyllo pastry with lemon custard."

Someone asked, "Why just one?"

"Because it's the best," our waiter answered.

He was right. After dinner, we sat back and relaxed. Piano music began in the largest room nearby as we savored a glass of *mirto* liqueur, another one of the owner's specialties, made from the berries of the myrtle bush. We had found our personal *acchiatura*, a treasure chest of food in a setting that represents Salento's history and culture—minus that pesky elf.

Luciana says: *The only wine museum in Salento is located on the first floor of* **Leone De Castris winery***, in the town of Salice Salentino. The museum shows the history of the family and the winery with photos, old bottles, documents, and ancient machines. Artistic and cultural events are often held in a lecture room in the museum. A guided tour takes you to the area where the wines are aged. Wine tasting is available.* Info: http://www.leonedecastris.com/tenute/#

POTATO AND MUSSEL CASSEROLE

Taieddhra

One afternoon, I sat with Luciana and her mother, Netta, in the living room of their summer house. Outside, the midday heat was reaching its peak but with closed shutters and a gleaming green-and-white tiled floor beneath our feet, we were comfortable. With Luciana translating, Netta described how she makes *taieddhra*, a traditional potato and mussel casserole.

She began, "Some southern Italians prefer to use rice along with potatoes, harking back to the time of Spanish rule in Salento, but I prefer potatoes alone. No rice, just potatoes." Aha! My first insight into understanding why Italians discuss food preparation while wading in warm, shallow seawater or standing amidst the ruins of the Roman Forum. Everyone has a different yet favorite way of making a dish and adamantly defending it.

A small discussion erupted over how much parsley was in a "handful," and what is a "good bit" of olive oil? A "pile" of mussels was even more challenging—with shells or without? Captured mussel water? My notes ran off the page as Luciana and her mother discussed the recipe. What's a "portion"? And when I expressed my doubts about opening mussels, Netta turned to Luciana and asked, "Doesn't everyone have a tool for opening mussels?" I haven't found one yet.

I learned that taieddhra is a popular dish for families throughout the heel of Italy's boot, but every family has its own way of preparing the dish. No one agrees on the spelling either—*tiella, taieddha, tajeddrha.* Netta's version, without rice, is a simple dish, characteristic of the area. In the spirit of this recipe, however, please feel free to make it your own by adding crushed red pepper, zucchini, sausage . . . or even rice.

In Salento, one is often served more than one small dish at a time. A Sunday meal may consist of several courses: taieddhra, beet salad, a zucchini frittata, pasta, and a meat dish, followed by fruit and dessert. Taieddrha may be served as a small dish accompanying other dishes. Serves 4 to 6.

Ingredients:
2 lbs small mussels in their shells, scrubbed clean and debearded
6–8 Yukon gold potatoes
¼ cup olive oil
1 cup Italian flat-leaf parsley leaves, minced and divided

1 cup breadcrumbs

1 cup clam juice (if more liquid needed)

½ cup dry white wine

4 tsp ground pepper, divided

Begin by preheating the oven to 350 degrees Fahrenheit.

Cut the potatoes into thin slices and arrange in layers in a 9 x 12 rectangular or oval baking dish.

Put the mussels in a large, deep, uncovered skillet with about ¼ cup of water, the wine, and the clam juice. Steam over medium-high heat, shaking the skillet intermittently, until the mussels open, about 3 to 5 minutes. Once the mussels have opened, drain the liquid through a strainer into a bowl. Discard any mussels that failed to open. To the liquid, add the olive oil, ½ of the ground pepper and ½ of the minced parsley. Mix well. You should end up with about 1½ cups of the mussel-clam liquid.

Pour about ½ cup of the liquid over the potatoes, just enough to thoroughly moisten them. Set the remaining liquid aside for later.

Bake the moistened potatoes in the oven until they are soft, about 45 minutes.

While the potatoes are baking, separate the mussel shells, preserving the attached mussels in their shells and discard the other half of the shells.

After the potatoes have baked and are soft, remove them from the oven and layer all of the mussels in their half-shells (mussel up) on top of the potatoes. Toss into the potato mixture any mussel that has separated from its shell.

Into the breadcrumbs mix the remaining ½ cup of minced parsley and the remaining 2 teaspoons of pepper.

Add a ½ teaspoon of the breadcrumb mixture to each mussel in its shell.

Spoon into each mussel shell a teaspoon of the remaining cup of mussel-clam liquid. Sprinkle any remaining liquid over the potatoes and mussels.

Put the casserole under a broiler for just a few minutes until a light crust has formed. Do not over-broil as the mussels and breadcrumbs will dry out quickly and burn.

Remove from the broiler and serve immediately.

CHAPTER FIVE

Lucia

THE COOK

A neighbor, Cummare (Godmother) Maria, rubbed me into life. It was November 16, 1955. I was a premature child, and the midwife had left me in a corner thinking I was dead, though all I needed was a warm hand on my back. A week later, my parents married. A few days after that a childless, married couple from the nearby town of Casarano asked my mother if they could adopt me. My father flatly refused. We were now a family.

Death's wings had brushed against me once, and they would come close again, in 1958, when Salento was overtaken by a polio epidemic. At that time there was no cure, no known remedy. During dark nights the ambulance sirens screamed throughout the town as sick people—most of them children— were taken to the hospital in the nearby city of Lecce, the only one equipped to handle the disease. Many didn't recover, and the ones who survived were paralyzed.

Lucia says: *Poliomyelitis, a contagious disease that was prevalent in Salento and elsewhere in the 1950s, struck thousands of people, mainly children. The disease affects the motor neurons of the spinal cord, causing paralysis. In 1958, the discovery and administration of the polio vaccine ended the scourge.*

One night, an ambulance arrived at our neighbor's door. My mother, gripped by fear and premonition, rushed into the bedroom where my three-year-old sister, Annarita, and I slept. She seized my feverish sister and tried to make her stand upright, but her legs collapsed beneath her. Annarita died a few days later. I had slept and spent every day with my sister but remained free of polio. I often wonder why.

I grew up in Taviano, where my family had become well known and popular. My mother and father were godparents or sponsors at baptisms and confirmations and witnesses at local weddings, too. Although it was a sign of the community's great respect for my parents, it meant that they were expected to help the godchildren and their families when help was needed. Neither family could fall in love with any of the family members of either side because people said, "There's Saint John between," which meant that the relationship was a tie that went beyond blood relatives. The whole family selected a godfather according to his wealth and character, a process not unlike a primary election.

An important ceremony, called *spasa*, occurred when a family consented to be godparents. The selected family was invited to the godchild's home where a large table of sweets was laid out: *taraddhi zuccarati*, circle-shaped biscuits covered with a white sugar icing; *pitteddhe*, simple round pastry sweets shaped like a small basket and filled with jam; and *mustazzoli*, brown, hard rhombus-shaped biscuits with cocoa, roasted almonds, and orange rind. These sweets were eaten on the spot with the leftovers given as gifts for the godfather's family.

My mother, father, a new baby named Annarita, after my three-year-old sister who had died, and

I were chosen as a godparent family by many families in Taviano and the surrounding towns. Looking back, I realize that we were well liked as a family because of my parents' good humor. My father, a very friendly person, is full of funny stories and jokes. Though he is an old man now, he is famous still for his card tricks. He is an honest and fair man whom everyone has relied on.

My mother, who passed away a few years ago, was a beautiful woman with dark hair and brown eyes. She loved to wear new coats, blouses, and skirts. A warm and communicative housewife, she was a wise advisor to her neighbors in any circumstance, always able to comfort and inspire during troubled times. She was even a good amateur nurse, if needed.

I remember one day when a neighbor had an accident as he was driving his three-wheeled Ape (small truck) home from an afternoon of farm work in his rural garden. He was badly bruised but his family did not know what to do to comfort him. The children were quiet and scared. The adults were stunned. My mother, aware that something was wrong, went to have a look to see what she could do.

She smiled and whispered, "It's nothing, it's nothing . . . Here, let's apply this ointment." At the same time she quickly put a big kettle on the stove, and in five minutes' time everyone in the room was drinking a cup of hot tea, and the children, sensing that the situation had changed for the better, returned to acting like their rambunctious selves, running around the room. It was as if an angel had flown down from heaven and made everything all right.

The interaction between my mother and my father was a continual succession of jokes and good humor about married life and funny events. What people liked best about them was their funny dialogue embedded in the mutual love and respect they had for each other.

My father is not very tall but he has a radiant, intelligent, and expressive face. He is a performer, and when on stage, that is, when he is telling jokes or performing magic tricks, he waits for the audience's reaction like a professional. He is also famous for his "double" walk—the normal one and the comical one where he bends slightly forward, shoulders rocking at each step, his hands in his trouser pockets. He walks this way when he leaves the room after a series of successful funny stories as a mark of personal satisfaction. But this is a mask, because I know that when he is alone he cries for my mother.

My father was called Messciu Pippi because he was a carpenter. All the craftsmen in Salento are called *Messciu*. As a carpenter, he was a *maestro d'ascia* (master of the hatchet). The title is addressed to those who keep the secrets of the craft, which are a "mystery." As a matter of fact, the Italian translation of "craft" is *mestiere*. My father used to tell me he had been tempted to steal the secrets of carpentry from his old master, who ordered all his apprentices to leave the workshop when he was going to make a particular joint or a wood interlocking system. After many years, on the threshold of retirement, the master revealed all his secrets to a chosen pupil, the only one destined to receive the secrets of the craft. That chosen pupil was my father.

With the secrets now known to him, he was able to open a workshop of his own. He began in the 1950s when the only instruments available to him were hand tools and the only raw materials were wood, nails, and glue. The work was like this: a young couple about to marry needed furniture for their new house. According to tradition, the bride's father had to buy the bedroom furniture. All the other furniture was the responsibility of the bridegroom's family. As the only furniture shop within a radius of fifty kilometers, all the furniture orders were given to my father, Messciu Pippi, often well in advance of the couple's marriage since it took him almost three months, after letting the wood season for at least one year, to make the various pieces, one by one, carving and polishing them by hand. It was a long and costly job and not the most efficient nor lucrative business.

One day, my father visited a trade fair a hundred kilometers to the north, in the city of Bari, where he saw for the first time a modern, hygienic, and washable piece of furniture made of chipboard and veneer. His eyes were opened. He could sense the future. He ordered the new materials and went to work: cut the boards—tens of them at the same time—assembled them and covered the pieces with a wood-grained laminate veneer called Formica. This process allowed him to mass-produce a lot of furniture in only one day. By this time, it was the 1960s, well after the war, and Italian industry was booming, which meant lots of products at a good price and lots of people able and eager to buy them.

In our little town of Taviano, for example, all the townsfolk became very willing to replace their traditional beds made of iron supports and wooden boards with the new veneer-covered ones produced by Messciu Pippi. It was my father's time as a successful entrepreneur; he assembled beds all day long and delivered them in the night. He bought a car and added a large sleeping area to our house. More importantly, he could afford the expenses of my school and university. I attended the University of Salento, in Lecce, and graduated in 1978 summa cum laude (highest honors) in Modern Languages. Now I teach English Literature in a high school in Gallipoli. My father had been in a position to make the social elevator climb up for me.

And when the elevator doors opened, Carlo, my future husband, was waiting for me. He was my tutor and my mentor. He guided me to my first teaching position, advising me to apply as a teacher of German so as to have a better chance at obtaining a job. Just as my life has been unpredictable from the start, the man that I married has not conformed to Italian societal expectations. He has been a tactful guide and friend to our two sons. He writes and plays his own music. He has always supported my teaching career.

Teaching literature is my life. I can teach it in so many different ways. I am always learning new things, especially from my students. Their comments about what they read are like rays of sunshine lighting the old texts. Literature has led me to reflect on my own life as it began so serendipitously; from Cummare Maria's warm, determined strokes to being a cherished child of loving parents in a community of neighbors and friends, and finally, to becoming a wife, mother, and teacher. Who could ask for anything more?

Audrey says: Alla Volta delle Stelle *is a small B&B in the southeastern Salento town of Corsano. The charming older home with vaulted ceilings is owned and run by Lucia's sister, Annarita, and her husband, Fabrizio. Annarita, a good cook like her sister, serves delicious homemade pastries for breakfast. Nearby you will find the scenic, rocky Adriatic coast with its hidden swimming spots. Fabrizio will be happy to show you where to go. Fabrizio and Annarita were guests at the open house hosted by Helen Mirren, the actress, and her film director husband, Taylor Hackford, to celebrate the purchase of their nearby masseria in the town of Tiggiano a number of years ago.* Info: www.allavoltadellestelle

BREAD AND OLIVE OIL

At the beginning, it was only white. The white cloud of the flour in the air of the high-ceilinged room and my grandmother in front of the open *mattrabbanca*—a table with a moving surface for the making and storage of bread—grading a heap of wheat. She used a round wooden tool, something like a tambourine, with a net in place of the center skin. The result of her work was the meal: simple light yellow meal. However, it was really all about my grandfather.

One of my first memories is of my grandfather carefully spreading a few drops of olive oil on a fragrant, still-warm slice of bread with his little finger. It was a slow, devout ceremony. He had known every single spike of wheat, watching it grow day by day and watching it bend in the field with the wind, always thinking of that supreme moment when he would taste the bread.

My grandfather made the bread himself; he was a baker. With flour and water on a special wooden board, his sleeves rolled up, he kneaded solemnly, making several loaves, each one a different size, according to its destination. Seven of them were for his daughters and their families, one for himself and Grandma, and the last one, which had been worked with special care—for his doctor. Dr. Pagliarulo was particularly fond of my grandfather's bread. He said there wasn't a way to get something like that from any of the numerous bakers in Caserano. Its smell, flavor, and consistency were unique. And it lasted almost two weeks without losing its mellowness. The recipe was a secret my grandfather revealed only to me, his favorite and first granddaughter.

He used to combine slowly wheat flour and warm water, salt, and yeast, kneading rigorously by hand and forming the dough. No one in the neighborhood bought yeast from the grocery store. Yeast was a common good. Every time you made your own bread, a small ball of leavened dough was saved up in a dish and a cross was drawn on it. It was called *llavatu*, and the cross, in addition to its religious meaning, was made to give the dough more air.

Every time the neighbors set out to make their own bread, they asked for the dish and used a small piece of the yeasty dough, saving a bit of it for the next ones, and so on. But before kneading, they had to tell the baker, my grandfather, to come to their houses to collect their loaves so he could bake them in his large oven. Since he started baking early in the morning, after bringing the oven to the right temperature by burning vine twigs and branches in it for a couple of hours, he called to the neighbors outside their houses in the dead of night crying, "*Tempara!*" Knead! After that, he came by and called again to collect the uncooked loaves on a wooden tray. On his bicycle, he balanced the bread-laden tray over one of his shoulders. You can't really imagine the smell of the warm bread rising in the fresh air of the day and spreading all over the village. It was such a consolation for the peasant heading off to hard work in the country.

Every morning, the usual meal of a peasant before leaving for the fields was the *cauteddhu*, a simple, nourishing soup eaten quickly on top of stale, homemade bread along with a glass of wine. It was made at daybreak by placing in a pot some onions, tomatoes dried up in the summer sun, chopped fresh tomatoes, crushed red pepper, a pinch of salt, some water, and olive oil; it cooked on low heat for about half an hour.

On that slice of bread my grandfather had baked, I spread olive oil and a thin layer of a homemade tomato cream called *strattu*. The making of it took a lot of time in summer. In July and August, my grandmother, along with some of her neighbors, used to collect a great deal of tomatoes, cutting and letting them drain their water overnight before sieving them one by one through a metal grater into a pot, sometimes with a few peppers. Then she added some basil and sugar and poured everything into a few enameled metal plates to be exposed to the sun on the roof terrace, a tulle veil laid on top to keep the flies away. She would stir the red sauce from time to time with a wooden spoon, but every day, before sunset, the plates had to be brought in to protect the precious sauce from the damp of the night.

You needed to work hard and be patient to obtain the final product, a dark red paste that could take the place of fresh tomatoes in the depths of winter. My granny just added salt and olive oil and put the *strattu* in glass jars sealed with a piece of cloth imbued with the same oil. At any time it was ready to be magically turned into a wonderful tomato sauce for pasta by just adding a glass of wine. That's what my grandpa used to put on his slice of bread!

A recent experience with bread and oil reminded me of my grandfather. My husband, our American friends, and I were sitting at an open-air restaurant in one of the beautiful, quiet, old town squares in Gallipoli. It was a warm summer evening, and all the shops were still open and illuminated. In front of us, the window of a fishmonger showed its sea treasures: bright pink mullets, spiny lobsters still alive with their shining nippers, and baskets full of cream-colored oysters that smelled of the sea. In this magical atmosphere, a woman appeared with a tray of tiny slices of bread and three glass cruets filled with green olive oil. She said that bread was the only way to appreciate the different qualities of oil that her company produced, so we should dip our bread into the three different oils and taste them.

In Salento, there are several varieties of olives. The most common are the *ciaddhine*, which are generally gathered from nets spread out under the olive trees where they fall when they are completely black and ripe. They are put into brine and take the name *ulie niure*, black olives. On the other hand, there are the so-called *ulie duci*, sweet olives; sweet but not as sweet as fruit. They are plucked directly from the tree branches when they are still green, so their taste is rather tart, becoming sweet only after being cured.

My grandmother cured them this way: she put the olives called *cazzarole* or *pasule* or *limoncelle* to soak in water for a couple of days. They had to be gathered no later than September. She changed their water two or three times. After crushing them with a wooden hammer or a meat hammer, she eliminated the stones and put layers of them into a special container, generally an enameled clay jar, along with oregano, garlic, green lemon skin, capers in brine, and salt. She left them for two days under a weight, such as a pot full of water, until their color turned dark. Then she poured off all the water and put the olives once and for all in layers in several glass jars with oil. Two years later, you could taste them, and they were always really sweet.

Audrey says: *I love ceramic pottery and while the tourist may run into small pottery shops in many of Salento's small towns, the best one we've found was shown to me by Annarita, the owner of the B&B Alla Volta delle Stelle. It is called* **Branca Ceramiche** *and is located in the town of Tricase, in the center of southern Salento. It has the best and largest selection of ceramics in the area. Also, workshops and classes are offered. You can design and make your own dish or pot.*
Info: https://www.facebook.com/agos.branca/

That night, at the restaurant in Gallipoli where we tasted the olive oil, the owner and producer of the oil, Mr. Adamo, talked with us. He told us that his family has owned more than one hundred olive trees for more than a century. He also owned an olive press so he could control the whole making of the product. We learned that the three cruets of olive oil we had tasted came from different kinds of olives and about the particular way of pressing them. He explained that the process involves the turning of special circular stones in a basin that crush the olives into a paste. Then the paste rests for about three hours, during which the oil rises up and is carefully collected with wooden spoons. This is the "oil flower," the purest, lightest, and most flavorful of the three varieties we tasted.

The second oil we tasted was the "extra virgin" olive oil. "To make this variety," Mr. Adamo's smiling wife explained, "we pick the olives from the trees when they are not yet fully ripe. That's how we get the fruity flavor you just tasted. The secret is crushing the olives only a few hours after they are picked. The paste serves as a natural fiber filter, and according to our traditional cold-pressing system, you don't need to use heat, which keeps the aroma and flavor natural and unadulterated."

By this time, thoroughly intrigued, we asked, "What about the third cruet?"

"This oil is a mixture of two different varieties of olives, *ogliarola* and *leccino*, harvested at maturity. If you smell it, you can sense a combination of green leaves and a slight aroma of tomato," said Mr. Adamo. "In my opinion, while tasting it you should even smell a bit of almond fragrance."

What I remember of that night, in addition to the flowery savor of the olive oils, was a fantastic first course of *tagliolini terra-mare*. The *tagliolini* are very thin, flat sheets of pasta dough made with eggs, so light and soft that they need a delicate sauce. Mrs. Adamo cooked the sauce. We could recognize squid, shrimp, champignon mushrooms, tomatoes, and parsley. But what was the missing ingredient? Something was hidden in the delicious mix. Mrs. Adamo realized from our puzzled expressions that we wanted to know more.

"We generally don't disclose anything about our recipes," she said with an amused smile. "But I can see how much you love cooking, so I'll make an exception to the rule. Here is how we do it: just put a bit of butter, a half-clove of garlic, squid, shrimps, and mushrooms in a saucepan and fry for a few seconds, sprinkling in a bit of brandy. Brown everything and add chopped tomatoes, a pinch of pepper and salt, and minced parsley. Then cook until everything blends together, add cream, and sauté everything in the saucepan. That's all. It's quick and simple."

In my mind, I remember Mrs.Adamo as if she were a fairy queen, wandering amongst the restaurant tables, talking to her customers and handing out joy—or was it simply the Salentinian wine employing its magic that summer evening in Gallipoli?

Lucia says: *The cutest restaurant in Gallipoli? It's* **La Puritate**, *with its view of the sea on a quiet lane in the old quarter of the city. You will love the hors d'oeuvres served on pineapple slices: small breaded mussels, rice salad with shrimp and almonds, and fried squid croquettes. Amazing! Taste the* mezzi-paccheri *(a wide, hollowed-out pasta tube that is a shorter version of* paccheri*) with shellfish, and the mussels sauté or the fillet of sea bass. The best ever. The waiters are careful and quick as lightning. Embroidered tablecloths, too.*
Info: www.lucianopignataro.it/a/gallipoli-salento-trattoria-la-puritate/28629/

LAND AND SEA TAGLIOLINI

Tagliolini terra-mare

The pasta in this recipe is like spaghetti only a bit thicker. It is common in Liguria, northern Italy, where Carlo, our music maker, was born. The land and sea part of this recipe represents the Spanish heritage of Lucia, our cook. Traditional Spanish paella has ingredients from the land and the sea. Tagiolini terra-mare follows suit. What could be more symbolic of Carlo and Lucia's marriage bond than a recipe that unites land and sea, southern Spain, and northern Italy? Serves 4.

Ingredients:
½ **lb squid, cleaned and chopped**
⅓ **lb shrimp, peeled**
1 cup fresh porcini (or your favorite) mushrooms, coarsely chopped
1 cup tomatoes, chopped
2 tbsp butter
1 tbsp cream
1 garlic clove, minced
Brandy to taste
Parsley, chopped
Salt and pepper
1 lb tagliolini pasta or spaghetti

Fill a large pot with water for the pasta, add a teaspoon of salt, and set on the heat to bring to a roiling boil.

In a separate deep skillet, place the butter, garlic, squid, shrimp, and mushrooms and sauté over medium heat for a minute or two.

Sprinkle lightly with brandy and add the chopped tomatoes, salt, pepper, and parsley, and cook (covered) over medium heat while you tend to the pasta.

Cook the pasta in the boiling water until it is *al dente* (firm—about 10 minutes for most dry pasta), drain and immediately add it to the skillet containing the squid and shrimp mixture. Stir in the pasta and the cream until mixed thoroughly and continue heating the entire dish until piping hot.

Serve immediately in individual pasta bowls, sprinkling each serving with a handful of parsley.

EASTER

At Easter time, we have something that is both symbolic and of substance: a lamb—neither alive nor dead—lying on a tray. It's a dessert made of almonds and sugar, a multicolored and fragrant work of art modeled not by a sculptor but by housewives who love and care for their children. The substance of the animal is ground almonds, both the sweet and bitter kind since, we Salentinians say, *lu troppu tuce stomaca*; that is, too much sweet can make you sick. This can also be said about excessive flattery.

One kilogram of crushed almonds is mixed with 700 grams of sugar and set aside. In a saucepan, more sugar (about 500 grams) is added along with half a liter of water and a few drops of lemon juice. The mixture is thickened over low heat. When it is thick enough, it is removed from the heat and the almond and sugar dough mixture is stirred in with a wooden spoon. The mixture is left to cool. When it has become firm, the dough is placed in a special lamb-shaped mold that, according to tradition, must be made of plaster.

My mother had her own lamb-shaped molds to be used at Easter and a fish-shaped one for Christmas, when the same kind of almond dough is made. The fish mold, like that of the lamb, is another symbol for Jesus Christ.

When the lamb is ready, each housewife adds her own decorations. My mother used chocolate and almonds to make a white and dark brown lamb. You almost expected it to bleat.

Lucia says: *Where can you find the best pastries in Salento? Many would say that you should go to Galatina, Maglie, or Lecce. In my opinion, the best* pasticiotto *(custard cake) in the area is made in Soleto, at the* **Caffé Euro***, on via Galatina. The custard inside is lemon flavored and as soft as butter. Yum!*
Info: http://indice.reteimprese.it/bar-caffe-euro-di-sambati-pietro-pasticceria-gelateria-soleto_943094

SAINT JOSEPH'S TABLE

Every year on March 19, the Festa di San Giuseppe (Feast of Saint Joseph), my mother would set the "Saint Joseph's Table" in front of a picture of the Holy Family. Like relatives and neighbors, she started cooking on the eve of the feast. The main course was *ciceri e tria*, a pasta and chickpea dish that recalls the pale yellow and gold colors of the narcissus flower that blooms in March in Salento. According to a legend, Saint Joseph had a narcissus flower attached to his walking stick.

Much of the food prepared for the Saint Joseph's Day Table is rich with religious symbolism. For example, a bowl of boiled cauliflower represents Saint Joseph's walking stick in blossom; fried fish and stewed codfish symbolize Jesus Christ; *lampascioni* (wild hyacinth bulbs) stand for the change from winter to spring; and *cartellate*, strips of fried dough sweetened with honey and nuts, popular at Christmas too, represent the infant Jesus's swaddling clothes.

Traditionally on this day, three people who are less fortunate than the hosts and who personify the Holy Family, are invited to lunch. The table is set with an immaculate tablecloth and three ring-shaped loaves of bread that encircle a fennel plant and an orange, all of which the guests will take with them at the end of the meal.

While watching my mother prepare our Saint Joseph's Table, I asked her to tell me what lunchtime was like when she was a child.

"Lucia, don't imagine anything like today's meals. The way we eat these days didn't exist. I mean, no starters, no first course, no second course, no side dish, no dessert; in a few words, no different dishes one after the other. I remember a single large dish in the middle of the table with everything in it and each member of the family taking bites. On special occasions, after this main and only course you would have some dried fruit or nuts or fennel and celery, along with a last glass of wine. There was also a sort of starter called *cumpanaggiu*, which means something eaten with bread, namely a slice of cheese or one sardine. Most days, this was the only way food was eaten . . . now pay attention to what I am doing."

My mother made the *tria* by kneading flour, water, and a pinch of salt into a thin sheet of pasta dough and cutting it into tiny strips. In the meantime, Granny cooked some chickpeas (*ciceri*) in an earthenware pot in the fireplace. Then she fried some *tria* (pasta strips) in a pan with olive oil to make the *frizzuli*, the fried pasta.

I remember our kitchen crammed with relatives busy with different tasks: reviving the fire, tasting the chickpeas, cutting more pasta strips. It was a joyful atmosphere filled with laughter and jokes. Both the *frizzuli* and the *ciceri* were added to the *tria* and the whole mixture cooked over low heat until the *tria* was ready. After sprinkling it with pepper, the dish was served hot to our guests.

Where did the Saint Joseph's Table tradition come from? Some say that a group of worshipers who believed in doing good works for others decided, as part of their mission to care for people, to prepare a meal for them on Saint Joseph's Day. It may also have emerged from the demands of the Byzantine liturgy ordering their monks to protect and feed poor people ravaged by illness and poverty. Others say that Albanian refugees introduced the tradition after fleeing to Salento from the Turks. Whatever the source, the Saint Joseph's Table is established in Salento as a day during which families, churches, and community organizations prepare and serve traditional foods for those who are less fortunate.

CHICKPEAS AND PASTA

Ciceri e tria

Even in areas where abundant wheat was cultivated, reaped, and milled, flour was considered a luxury. It was used primarily to make bread, an essential element of the Salento family's daily fare—*frise* and *taralli*, crispy baked dough, which could be preserved for days and be eaten when nothing fresh was available; and, of course, fresh-made pasta: *orecchiette, minchiareddhri, sagne ritorte, tria*, all symbols of the Salento diet.

Many typical local dishes include breadcrumbs, fried bread, or pasta. Why? Because they were meant to mimic the texture of meat back when it was difficult to come by. This seemed to work well for children, both in the past and now. "Chickpeas and pasta" is a favorite local dish—substantial yet meatless, peasant food with a fancy twist. When you have nothing, you invent. This is a classic example of how the Salento cook becomes an alchemist. Serves 6.

"Ciceri e tria, ciceri e tria quista ete la pasta te la terra mia."
Chickpeas and tria, chickpeas and tria, this is the pasta from my land.

Ingredients

For the tria:
4 cups durum or a mix of durum and wheat flour
1 cup warm water
2 tsp salt
Extra virgin olive oil (for deep frying)

For the chickpeas:
2¼ cups dried chickpeas
2 tbsp baking soda
1 celery stalk
1 garlic clove
2 bay leaves

A sprig of parsley
Extra virgin olive oil
1 medium tomato, peeled
1 medium carrot
Salt
Fresh or dried red chili pepper

Making the tria

Dissolve the salt into the warm water. Put most of the flour on a work surface or into a mixing bowl. Make a well in the center. Add the salted water very slowly while mixing constantly with a wooden spoon. Add more warm water, if needed. After a few minutes, move the dough to a lightly floured work surface to avoid sticking. Knead, working in small amounts of the remaining flour as needed, for about 10 minutes until the dough becomes very smooth and soft but not damp or sticky. Form a ball and wrap dough in a towel to rest for 30 minutes.

When the dough is ready, take it out and begin rolling it out into a circle (as if making pizza). Once the dough is thin enough, roll it around the rolling pin and continue rolling until you end up with a sheet of pasta almost paper-thin. Flatten the sheet and roll into a log. Slice the log into a bit less than ½-inch strands. Then open up the strands by fluttering your fingers through them. Set the tria on a flour-sprinkled surface. Allow to dry for several hours.

Preparing the chickpeas

Place the chickpeas in a large bowl and cover them generously with cold water and 2 tablespoons of baking soda. Soak for at least 8 hours or overnight.

Drain and rinse the chickpeas. Place them in a large, heavy pot and cover with fresh water. Add the onion, carrot, celery, tomato, bay leaves, and garlic. Bring to a boil, add salt, cover the pan, and let them simmer for about an hour or until the chickpeas become very tender, adding more water from time to time, if needed.

Cooking the Tria

Set a large covered pot of salted water over high heat.

Meanwhile, fill a deep pot with olive oil. Heat and carefully place about ¼ of the tria into the hot oil, separating the strands as much as possible. Fry for 1 to 2 minutes until crisp and brown, the so-called "*frizzuli*" (fried tria). Remove the strands and set aside on a paper-towel-lined tray.

When the water boils, carefully add the remaining tria, separating the strands as much as possible. Stir to separate and boil for about 2 minutes (quite *al dente*). Drain.

Keep the chickpeas hot over low heat. Remove the bay leaves and other vegetables used during the cooking from the chickpeas and discard. Add the boiled tria and the frizzuli to the chickpeas just minutes before serving. Stir gently. Garnish with fresh parsley and season to taste with either fresh or dried red chili pepper.

CHRISTMAS SWEETS

Every year, I knew when it was Christmastime. The atmosphere of my house felt thick and, how do you say, spicy but at the same time sweet. Opening my bedroom window to the cold air, I could hear the rapid, happy tolling of bells, the signal to get up and get into a kitchen that would soon be enveloped in the fragrance of herbs and fried oil. I remember that everything in the kitchen was clean and shiny because that is the way my mother cooked. She washed every utensil after using it so it could be used again. She fried in the oil only once. The kitchen air was fresh and magical, for I was a little girl at the time.

On the table were eggs, lemons, oranges, candied citron peel, honey in a glass jar, and olive oil in a shiny aluminum cruet. Everything was within reach of my mother's arms—everything she needed for *purciaddhuzzi* (sweets). At Christmas we had several kinds because all the neighbors and relatives were proud of their own versions. At the end of the meal we had three or four dishes of *purciaddhuzzi*, one made by Cummare Picia, another made by Cummare Ntunietta, and so on. So there I was, a few days before Christmas, leaning against the table, my eyes at the same level as my mother's hands, watching her while she made her own version of a famous local sweet.

My mother filled the hole in the heap of flour with eggs, lard, sugar, salt, and chopped lemon peel. Her hands rolled—no, what's the word, kneaded everything as if it were child's play, shaping several strands of pasta, cutting them into three-centimeters-long pieces. But there was also an artistic element as she carved each one and rolled it on the straw weft of a handmade basket, the imprint turning it into a small jewel. Then she fried these jewels in olive oil. The result was a multitude of warm, golden sticks. But the process was not finished.

Into a saucepan with melted honey and grated orange peel, she stirred and dropped the sticks one by one so that each one bathed in a coat of honey. The finishing touches were a few tiny multicolored sprinkles of sugar on top. Imagine me as a child standing there before the glittering heap, hypnotized by the colors and smells, waiting to taste the soft pastry when suddenly my mother decapitated the sweet heap and scooped it into a new dish. "Take this to Cummare Picia so she can see how our *purciaddhuzzi* have turned out!"

Another traditional and popular sweet are the *chinuliddhe*, meaning "stuffed things." They are made of a doubled-dough "jacket" stuffed with jam or ricotta and then fried. Eventually they are covered with honey or cinnamon frosting. According to tradition, they symbolize the pillow on which the baby Jesus rested his head.

Midday was still far off, so my mother, after cleaning wooden spoons, white-and-blue bowls, and saucepans, began another delicious operation: the making of *pittule*, a simple food made of flour, salt, and yeast, our traditional fritters. I was particularly fond of them since they are best if eaten soon after they are pulled out of the frying pan, hot and fragrant. I didn't have to wait until lunchtime to taste them.

My mother put these ingredients into a tureen of warm water, mixing them slowly with her hands until a soft, almost runny dough formed. While the dough was rising, we went to church, because my mother thought the *pittule* tasted better after the service. The cooking part began. She poured spoonfuls of the dough directly into the hot olive oil, and from the pan a host of puffy, round flowers rose to the oil's surface, like magic. She sometimes mixed the dough with cauliflower, anchovy, cod, or *nsirnia*, a type of wild celery. The result was hot, fragrant fritters with a variety of flavors and aromas.

Certain beliefs accompanied this traditional holiday cooking. For example, housewives had to cook *pittule* and *purciaddhuzzi* only from midnight to dawn on Christmas Eve in order not to commit a sin. Of course, there were thousands of sins worse than this. Also, the cook had to cut a bit from the last fritter to be fried and throw it into the fireplace as a good omen after saying a prayer. If the fritters had to be moved from one dish to another, it was advisable to leave at least one *pittula* in the previous dish to prevent all the fritters from going bad.

Lucia says: *How would you like to eat a meal in a restaurant where author Andrea Camilleri's fictional character Inspector Montalbano would be comfortable? The place is* **La Fulana Trattoria,** *in the town of Giuliano. Philosophers' portraits decorate the walls. All food ingredients come from the surrounding countryside. You can savor the traditional Salento dishes, such as* sagne *(a type of pasta) with ricotta; orechiette with tomatoes, arugula, and sausage; or croquettes with tomato sauce. Be sure to try the dessert cake made with pears and almonds.*
Info: www.fulanatrattoria.it

PUDDING CAKE (WITH CREAM OR JAM)

Pasticciotto con crema pasticcera
o marmellata

Salento is known for its cream-filled pastries. The pudding cake is famous. So it was important that I, as editor of our book, get together with Lucia and Luciana one morning to watch Lucia make it. My job was to watch and write the recipe. It sounded simple enough. Writing down the number of eggs was easy. The problems began with sugar.

Me: Wait, Lucia . . . how much sugar did you just put in?

Lucia: Just a little bit . . .

Me: How much is "a little bit"?

Lucia (cupping her fist): About this much?

Me: A tablespoon, perhaps?

Lucia: What's a tablespoon?

It was time for Luciana to step in and translate for us: amounts into grams into tablespoons and teaspoons. Back and forth, repeat and repeat again, not to mention the side arguments about what was best: this flour or that, whole milk or skim, small eggs or large. But we made it to the end, or almost to the end. The dessert was removed from the oven and set on the counter to cool while we enjoyed numerous dishes for lunch and tasted three different wines. We had so much fun eating, drinking, and talking that we forgot about the cooling cream cake dessert on the kitchen counter! Perhaps it was best that way—a fresh cream cake would be waiting for us next year!

Ingredients for the cream*:

2 eggs

2 tbsp sugar

2 tbsp flour

1–2 tsp grated lemon peel

2¼ cups whole milk

Combine ingredients in a saucepan over medium heat, stirring constantly until the mixture is thick and you can see the bottom of the pan during the stir strokes.

Set the cream aside.

Ingredients for the cake:
4 cups pastry flour
1 cup sugar
Pinch of salt
3 tsp baking powder
4 eggs, beaten
1 cup melted butter

Preheat the oven to 350 degrees Fahrenheit.

Combine the dry ingredients in a large bowl.

Make a hole in the center of the dry ingredients and add the melted butter and the beaten eggs.

Mix these ingredients until they have a bread-like consistency, then knead the dough. If the dough feels too sticky, add more flour until it holds together.

Refrigerate the dough until it is chilled.

Lightly flour a round or square baking dish.

Take ½ of the chilled dough and pat it into the shape of the baking dish or pan (going up the sides) to form a crust of about ¼- to ½-inch in thickness.

Pour the cream into the crust.

Roll out the remaining dough and place it on top of the layer of cream.* Lightly sprinkle sugar on top of the pastry.

Bake for 30 minutes or so until the surface turns a light brown.

*Our friends often substitute a fruit jam filling in place of the cream. If you do this, roll out the dough for the top pastry layer and cut it into strips; crisscross the strips over the jam filling. Baking time and oven temperature remain the same.

Back and Forth in Memory

We compose our lives in time, improvising and responding to context, yet weaving threads of continuity and connecting the whole as we move back and forth in memory.
—Mary Catherine Bateson, *Composing a Further Life: The Age of Active Wisdom*

As editor and an author of **SALENTO BY 5**, I searched for stories, patterns, and information that would capture a reader's curiosity about Salento, as mine had been caught so many years ago. Gathering the material from afar presented the obvious difficulties but in the end, the greater challenge was that of finding a format that would best convey the excitement of travel, friendship, and storytelling by more than one author.

When the project began, my ninety-year-old mother was active and well. As her health declined with age, I was able to visit Salento yearly but not without worry. Luckily, my notes of early trips to southern Italy and my husband's sketches drew me back to my writing desk as I searched for what was so enticing about the place and its people. What was it, really, that made us return to the same place year after year?

Once we and our Italian friends decided to write a book together, we thought email would provide for frequent and easy communication. But it was our face-to-face meetings in Italy that were by far the most productive. Progress was slow. How could we keep up momentum and interest in the book? On every visit, my suitcase was filled with illustrated samples of the stories we each had contributed to the effort, and once we arrived, we'd spend time reading and responding to the work, laying out elaborate timelines for future pieces. I worried about the book's progress, especially when I was home. Was it feasible? How committed were our Italian friends? Did they want to be friends with us still or were we viewed only as those American tourists back again to disturb their tranquil summers? My worries were unfounded. After each trip, I was always reassured, grateful, and excited about its progress. "Yes, it would take time, but it was coming along" became our mantra.

While time was in our favor for the book project, time was also taking its toll on my mother's health as she began to fail. Leaving her for any extended time became difficult. She began to lose touch with reality and eventually could no longer live independently. We found a home for her care, and on a day not long before she died, we sat together in the living room, drinking coffee and eating doughnuts.

My mom said, "What are you doing these days? I haven't seen you in a while." She paused. "I haven't seen my daughter in a while either."

"But I am your daughter!" I responded. "I'm writing a book!"

"No, you just sound like her. She's writing a book too."

I smiled. At least I existed—and so did the book!

The book is now complete. It found its form. What seemed such a shapeless mass has metamorphosed into a travel memoir by five authors, thanks to the thoughtful support of friends and colleagues.

As the shape of the book evolved, earlier versions were tossed aside. We moved on, discarding, revising. And while we were at home in the States, Salento moved on too. Our Otranto apartment was outfitted with a new terrace overhang made of solid wood. The howling sirocco, maestrale, or tramontana winds would no longer tear at bamboo curtains and keep us awake at night. The bathtub was replaced with a tiled shower. Carlo retired from teaching. Luciana completed an additional teaching certificate program. Now she teaches physically and mentally challenged students. Tullio, her father, passed away. Netta, his wife, misses him terribly. Lucia continues to teach English literature and keeps us well fed whenever we visit. Her father, now in his eighties, entertains us *americani* as usual, with card tricks, jokes, and a friendly smile.

The coffee bar by the sea in Otranto where fishermen and local policemen would gather for early morning coffee and gossip has become a fast-food restaurant. Bibbò, the owner, said he would make more money that way. The Wednesday morning market held in the central park now sprawls across an empty lot on the town's outskirts. A small bus travels back and forth from the market, up past the historic center, and on to the other side of town. It is fun to stand in line for the bus with the women shoppers and talk about food and recipes. A new disco bar has opened on the cement pier where we swim, forcing us to make our way to the steps at the end of the pier through cushioned chairs, glass-topped cocktail tables, and loudspeakers blasting rock 'n' roll. A new four-lane highway leading into town will soon replace the present two-lane road. Gone are the century-old olive trees that once marched alongside. When we express our dismay, some Otrantini agree and have protested the tree removal. But the majority are resigned and tell us it will be a good thing—it will cut down on the frequent accidents involving cars and scooters as a growing number of visitors, both foreign and Italian, head to and from the Otranto coast.

We ask ourselves, Will Otranto become too much a Disneyland of gift shops and fried-food emporiums? Will the Otrantini protest the ear-splitting electric buzzes and booms reverberating off castle walls during late-night music extravaganzas? Is this progress? What about the litter abandoned at seaside swimming spots?

"The summers are the worst," says Francesca, my Otrantina Italian teacher. "When tourists leave, we take back our town by the sea. Most of the restaurants and tourist shops close or cut back their hours." Residents who have rented out their homes in the historic center to tourists return from their summer country houses and move back into their Otranto homes. The sea gets cold. Storms blow in and out, carrying away the summer trash and much of the beach sand too.

But every year, by June, the sand is back in place, new flowers are blooming in large pots along the walkways, and bright umbrellas line the beaches. New recycling bins are everywhere. And although an old favorite restaurant may have closed, new ones have opened.

On a warm night, the first of our visit just last year, we heard thrumming tambourines, singing, and handclapping as we walked along the promenade by the sea. An impromptu concert of local tambourine talent had begun outside a popular coffee bar. Music, laughter, and local songs in dialect drew a crowd. With warm breezes behind us, a full moon rising, soft waves breaking on the shore, we moved in closer and joined the clapping as musical stories of lost love, strong women, and hardworking peasants soared into the night. Music, language, and history, the sea and the people—this was and still is our Salento.

Carlo said not to write an epilogue because it would mean the end of the project and no one likes endings. But now that we have a book to share, why not think of it as a **beginning**? More sharing. More stories. We invite you, dear reader, to join us virtually. Please visit our website, www.SALENTOby5.com, to read our updated blogs. And for those of you fortunate enough to find yourselves in Salento, as either residents or visitors, we invite you to share your experiences online at our website Comments section.

—Audrey Fielding

olive trees and muri secchi

"We travel, initially, to lose ourselves; and we travel, next to find ourselves. We travel to open our hearts and eyes and learn more about the world than our newspapers will accommodate. We travel to bring what little we can, in our ignorance and knowledge, to those parts of the globe whose riches are differently dispersed. And we travel, in essence, to become young fools again—to slow time down and get taken in, and fall in love once more."

—Pico Iyer

ACKNOWLEDGMENTS

On behalf of all five authors, we wish to acknowledge and thank Kari Hock, Gemelli Press publisher, and Michelle Fabio, our editor, for their enthusiastic support of *Salento by 5*. When we first discovered the existence of Gemelli Press, with its website proclaiming twin passions for books and Italy, we were cautiously excited about the possibility that they would like our manuscript. Would a collaboration between American travelers and newfound Italian friends on a book about a relatively remote corner of southern Italy interest them? You can imagine our collective thrill when Kari responded enthusiastically and readily launched the process of bringing our book to publication. From all of us, thank you to Gemelli for your unwavering support.

We thank our Italian co-authors from Taviano, their families, and friends for sharing their lives so generously. Without them, this special journey would not have been realized.

Finally, we thank our family, friends, and colleagues for their gentle but persistent prodding—"How's the book?" They kept us on task when it would have been easy to let the project slip away. They helped us find a way to capture and preserve our love for the Salento and its people.

Audrey and David Fielding

INDEX OF AUTHOR RECOMMENDATIONS